Dave Grohl
Autobiography

STORYTELLER OF ROCK

Matthew Paul Belanger

TABLE OF CONTENTS

INTRODUCTION: TURN IT UP

PART 1: SETTING THE SCENE

DNA DOESN'T LIE

THE HEARTBREAK OF SANDI

THE SCARS ARE ON THE INSIDE

JOHN BONHAM SÉANCE

PART 2: THE BUILDUP

YOU'D BETTER BE GOOD

EVERY DAY IS A BLANK PAGE

IT'S A FOREVER THING

WE WERE SURROUNDED AND THERE WAS NO WAY OUT

PART 3: THE MOMENT

HE'S GONE

THE HEARTBREAKER

THIS IS WHAT I WANTED

PART 4: CRUISING

CROSSING THE BRIDGE TO WASHINGTON

LIFE WAS PICKING UP SPEED

INSPIRED, YET AGAIN

PART 5: LIVING

BEDTIME STORIES WITH JOAN JETT

THE DADDY-DAUGHTER DANCE

THE WISDOM OF VIOLET

CONCLUSION: ANOTHER STEP IN THE CROSSWALK

INTRODUCTION

TURN IT UP

I sometimes forget how much I've aged.

My mind and heart appear to play a terrible joke on me, tricking me with the false illusion of youth by welcoming the world every day through the idealistic, mischievous eyes of a rebellious child who finds delight and admiration in the most basic, simple things.

It just takes a quick glance in the mirror to tell me that I am no longer the small boy with a cheap guitar and a stack of albums, practicing alone for hours on end in the hopes of one day breaking free from the limits and expectations of his suburban Virginia, Wonder Bread existence. No. My reflection now shows the chipped teeth of a worn smile, cracked and shortened by years of microphones grinding away at their fragile enamel. I can see the huge bags under my hooded eyes from decades of jet lag, forsaking sleep for another precious hour of life. I see white patches in my beard. And I am grateful for all of it.

Years ago, I was invited to perform at the 12-12-12 Hurricane Sandy charity event in New York City. It took place in Madison Square Garden and featured the Mount Rushmore of rock and roll lineups, including McCartney, the Rolling Stones, the Who, Roger Waters, and countless more household names. At one point, a promoter approached me and asked if I would join some of these most legendary artists in the greenroom to take photos with fans who had donated enormous quantities of money to the cause. Honored to be involved, I readily consented and made my way through the maze of backstage passages, visualizing a room full of rock and roll history, all dressed in leather jackets and British accents for an elementary school portrait. As I entered, I was astonished to see only two performers standing at opposite ends of the room. One had the gleaming appearance of a brand-new luxury vehicle. Perfectly dyed hair, spray tan, and a newly refurbished smile that resembled a fresh box of Chiclets (an obvious attempt to ward off the aging process, which eventually had the opposite effect, giving the appearance of an ancient wall with too many layers of paint). The other has the appearance of an old, burned-out hot rod. Wiry gray hair, deep lines chiseled into a scowl, teeth that could have belonged to George Washington, and a black T-shirt hugging a barrel-chested frame so tightly, you knew right once that this was someone who didn't give a flying fuck.

Epiphany may sound cliché, but in a flash, I saw my destiny. I decided right there that I would become the latter. That I would celebrate the coming years by accepting the toll they would exact on me. That I would aspire to be the rusted-out hot rod, regardless of how many jump-starts I needed along the road. Not everything requires a shine, after all. If you leave a Pelham Blue Gibson Trini Lopez guitar in its case for fifty years, it will still look brand new. However, if you hold it in your hands, expose it to the light, allow it to breathe, sweat on it, and PLAY with it, the finish will change over time. And every instrument matures differently. To me, that is beauty. Not the sparkle of manufactured perfection, but the weathered beauty of uniqueness, time, and wisdom.

Miraculously, my memory has been pretty intact. Since I was a child, I've measured my existence in musical units rather than months or years. My memory relies on songs, albums, and bands to recall a specific moment and location. Some people recall memories by taste, whereas others recall them through sight or smell. Mine is activated by sound and plays like an unfinished mixtape ready to be sent.

Though I have never been one to accumulate "stuff," I do collect memories. I've tried my best to capture some of them in this book. Of course, these recollections from my entire life are filled with music. They can be loud at times. ***Turn it up. LISTEN WITH ME.***

PART 1

SETTING THE SCENE

DNA DOESN'T LIE

"Dad, I want to learn how to play the drums."

I knew it was coming.

Harper, my eight-year-old daughter, stood there, peering at me with large brown eyes like Cindy Lou Who from How the Grinch Stole Christmas and anxiously holding a pair of my shattered drumsticks in her tiny little hands. My middle child, my mini-me, the girl who looks most like me. I knew she'd be interested in music eventually, but drums? What a low-paying, entry-level mailroom position!

"Drums?" I responded with raised eyebrows.

"Yeah!" she said through a toothy grin. I took a minute to reflect, and as an emotional knot formed in my throat, I responded, "Okay... and you want me to teach you?" Shifting in her checkered Vans sneakers, she sheepishly nodded and muttered, "Uh-huh," eliciting a rush of fatherly pride and a huge smile from me. We hugged and walked upstairs together to the old drum equipment in my office. This is a memory that I will love forever, like a weepy Hallmark moment from one of those hyper emotional Super Bowl commercials (the ones that would leave even the most ardent monster truck fan crying in their buffalo chicken dip).

The moment we walked into my office, I remembered that I had never had official drum lessons, therefore I had no idea how to teach someone to play. The closest I had ever gotten to systematic music training was a few hours with an exceptional jazz drummer named

Lenny Robinson, whom I used to see perform every Sunday afternoon at a little Washington, DC jazz club called One Step Down. One Step Down, a tiny old club on Pennsylvania Avenue just outside of Georgetown, was not only a hotspot for established touring acts, but it also hosted a jazz workshop every weekend, with the house band (led by DC jazz legend Lawrence Wheatley) performing a few sets to the dark, crowded room and then inviting up-and-coming musicians to jam with them onstage. When I was a teenager in the 1980s, those classes became a Sunday tradition for my mother and me. We'd sit at a small table, buy drinks and appetizers, and watch these musical masters play for hours, soaking up the beautiful, spontaneous freedom of traditional jazz. You never knew what to expect within those bare brick walls, with smoke hanging in the air and the only sound coming from the small stage (talking was absolutely forbidden). At the time, I was fifteen years old and obsessed with punk rock, listening to only the loudest, quickest music I could find, but I felt a connection to the emotional qualities of jazz. Unlike the conventions of modern music (which I despised at the time, much like the kid from The Omen in church), I found beauty and vitality in the chaotic tapestry of jazz composition. Sometimes structured, sometimes unstructured. But most of all, I adored Lenny Robinson's drumming. This was something I'd never seen before at a punk rock concert. Thunderous expression with exquisite accuracy; he made it all appear so simple (I now know it wasn't). It was a kind of musical revelation for me. I'd trained myself to play the drums by ear on soiled pillows in my bedroom, and I'd never had somebody standing over me telling me what was "right" or "wrong," so my drumming was erratic and feral. I WAS AN ANIMAL FROM THE MUPPETS, WITHOUT THE CHOPS. Lenny clearly had some training, and I was impressed by his feel and control. My "teachers" back then were my punk rock records: rapid, discordant, screaming slabs of noisy vinyl, with drummers that most would not consider traditional, but their crude brilliance was unmistakable, and I will always be grateful to these unsung giants of the underground punk rock scene.

"Okay, yeah... here is the kick drum. "Your foot goes there," I remarked, as Harper's small sneaker sat on the bass pedal. "This is your hi-hat; your other foot goes there." She relaxed into her perch, sticks in hand, and prepared to whale. Without knowing what I was doing, I skipped over all of the ridiculous right-left-right-left nonsense that Lenny Robinson had shown me (all respect, Lenny) and went straight to teaching her a beat. "Ummm . . . okay . . . here's a simple kick-snare pattern . . ." After a few frustrated attempts, I stopped her and told her to wait. I raced out of the room, saying, "I'll be right back." I understood exactly what she needed. It was not me. It was AC/DC's Back in Black.

I turned on the title track and instructed her to listen. "Hear that?" I asked. "That is the kick drum." And that is the hi-hat. "And that is the snare drum." She listened carefully and began to play. Her time was impeccable, which any drummer understands is more than half the battle. She had a natural, built-in meter, and after she mastered the coordination of her motions, she began playing with incredible feel. I jumped and cheered as my heart swelled with joy, headbanging and sang along to the songs while Harper performed. Then something unusual occurred to me: her stance. Her broad back arched forward somewhat, angular arms and narrow elbows extended slightly, chin elevated over the snare... and I saw it. She was a mirror image of myself playing the drums when I was her age. I felt like I was traveling through time and having an out-of-body experience all at once. Not only that, but here was my mini-me, my smiling twin, learning to play the drums the same way I had thirty-five years before: by listening to music with her parents. I wasn't surprised, however. As I previously stated, I had anticipated this outcome.

As I stated in the foreword to my mother's book, From Cradle to Stage, I believe that these musical impulses are programmed and exist somewhere deep within the DNA strand, ready to be awakened.

I stated, "DNA is a miraculous thing. We all have traits from people we've never met somewhere deep within our chemistry. I am not a scientist, but I believe my musical abilities are proof of this. There is no divine involvement here. This is made of flesh and blood. Someone created these ears, hearts, and minds. Someone who shared my passion for music and song. I was endowed with a genetic symphony waiting to be performed. All it took was a spark.

Harper's "spark" had arrived the day before, as she sat in her seat at the Roxy nightclub on Sunset Boulevard, watching her older sister, Violet, perform her debut concert at the age of eleven.

Yes, I was expecting that one as well.

Violet was a very vocal child. By the age of three, she was speaking with the fluency and language of a much older child, frequently surprising unsuspecting servers at restaurants from her booster seat with properly enunciated requests like "Excuse me, sir?" Could I perhaps have more butter with my bread?" (I peed my pants laughing every time, watching folks do a double take as if we were a weird ventriloquist show.) When she was throwing a tantrum over something at the dinner table, I tried to calm her down by saying, "Look, it's okay; everyone gets upset sometimes. Even I get irritated!" She replied, "I'm not angry! "I'm just frustrated!" (I still don't understand the distinction, but Violet knows.) I eventually found she had a great aural recall and a keen sense of pattern recognition, allowing her to accurately reproduce or repeat things by ear. That quickly evolved to doing accents on demand, where she would run through spot-on impersonations of an Irish person, a Scottish person, an English person, an Italian person, and so on, all before she ever got out of her smoothie-stained vehicle seat.

Violet's love of music soon honed her sense of pitch, key, and tone. As she sang from the back seat, I could hear her focusing on the tiny movements of her favorite singers' voices. The Beatles' harmonies,

Freddie Mercury's vibrato, Amy Winehouse's soul (probably the most memorable, since nothing beats hearing your five-year-old kid sing "Rehab" word for word while dressed in Yo Gabba Gabba! pajamas). It was evident that she possessed the gift. Now it was only a matter of time before she discovered the spark.

That spark grew into a wildfire, and music became her life's divining rod, eventually leading her to create a rock band with her peers. She grew stronger and more confident with each performance, with a ravenous and delightfully eclectic ear for music, singing along to anything from Aretha Franklin to the Ramones, broadening her range as she embarked on a journey of discovery and inspiration. Her genetic symphony was performing, and all we could do was sit back and listen. After all, this is something that begins on the inside.

Violet's first "official" show with her band was at the Roxy on Sunset Boulevard, and I sat in the audience with my family while she sang her set. My personal favorites were "Don't Stop Believin'" by Journey, "Hit Me with Your Best Shot" by Pat Benatar, and "Sweet Child O' Mine" by Guns N' Roses, although I had to pause throughout the performance to enjoy the moment. Harper's eyes were filled with thoughts of being a singer someday, while my mother was happily witnessing another generation of her family baring their souls in front of a room full of strangers. It was a remarkable event, best summed up in an email my mother wrote the next day that said, "Now YOU know what it's like to nervously sit in an audience as YOUR child steps onstage for the first time to follow their life passion with a funny haircut, dressed in jeans and a t-shirt." She was correct. THIS WAS NOT DIVINE INTERVENTION. This was flesh and blood.

Since then, I've performed with both of my children in front of thousands of people all around the world, and each time, I'm filled with the same pride that my mother felt on that muggy July afternoon at One Step Down so many years ago. I am inspired by my children's bravery and hope that their children will feel the same joy and echo my words from my mother's book: "But, beyond any biological information, there is love." Something that defies both science and logic. And I consider myself quite fortunate to have received this. It's perhaps the most defining factor in anyone's life. Certainly an artist's greatest muse. There is no love like a mother's. It's life's finest song. We are all grateful to the women who gave us life. Music would not exist without them."

THE HEARTBREAK OF SANDI

Her name was Sandi.

And she was my first heartbreak.

It was 1982, and as a gangly thirteen-year-old starting seventh grade, I was overcome with apprehensive excitement at meeting all of the new, strange individuals at Holmes Intermediate School. Until that moment, my life had been confined to my quaint little North Springfield neighborhood, where I had grown up with the same kids since kindergarten in our suburban maze of rolling hills and congested cul-de-sacs. North Springfield, located just twelve miles south of Washington, DC, was little more than a rural crossroads until it was subdivided in the late 1950s and early 1960s, resulting in twisting lanes dotted with modest, cookie-cutter brick homes. The American Dream. Where I grew up, there were only three sorts of houses: the one-level econo-model, the split-level Brady Bunch model, and the two-story mac-daddy party crib (all under 1,700 square feet) built on tiny lots, yard after yard. Make a wild guess which one I lived in. That's right, it's all about the economy, baby. With three bedrooms and one bathroom, my mother could comfortably raise two children on her low Fairfax County Public Schools salary. We did not have much, but we always had enough. North Springfield was a close-knit community of largely young families; there were no true strangers there. It was a town where everyone knew your name, which street you lived on, and which church you went to after your messy divorce. Each block had its own gang of scruffy hoodlums who terrorized the otherwise friendly sidewalks (mine included), and I spent my childhood climbing trees, chewing tobacco, playing hooky, setting off firecrackers, searching the creeks for crawfish, and spray-painting walls alongside the best of them. This was pure seventies Americana shit—a faded Kodachrome portrait brought to life. Banana seat bikes and BB pistols. A life somewhere between Rob Reiner's Stand by Me and Tim Hunter's timeless River's Edge.

The notion of attending another school with students from various, remote neighborhoods seemed almost international to me. My entire life, I had walked the single block to my elementary school, which was located around the corner. However, I had carefully planned for the next step. With a couple new shirts from the bargain fashion retailers off the Pennsylvania Turnpike and a fresh bottle of Old Spice, I was excited to expand out and finally discover my niche. Maybe I'll meet my suburban soul mate beneath the fluorescent lights of my new school's locker-lined hallways. I'd never been in love, but I knew she was out there somewhere.

Every day, I boarded the bus with a big plastic comb stuffed into the back pocket of my corduroy pants and dusty Nike sneakers, hoping to make it to the final bell without getting kicked or expelled. I was a fucking terrible student, and I was already in the early phases of my punk rock chrysalis, having heard the B-52s and Devo on Saturday Night Live and somehow relating to the subversive, radical aesthetic of their music, so I was taking baby steps in the background. As much as I wanted to fit in and be accepted. I felt different deep down inside my circle of friends. It would be years before I discovered the guts to accept my uniqueness, but at the time, I was almost closed off, suppressing my love of alternative culture for fear of being rejected by the cool kids. I joined in, I suppose, but I knew I wasn't made out for the Key Club or the football team. I was a misfit, seeking to be understood and accepted for who I truly was.

And then I saw her.

Sandi was the most stunning girl I'd ever seen. Ice-blue eyes, feathery blond hair, and a smile so bright it could have charged every Tesla from Brentwood to Beijing, if Teslas existed in 1982. Farrah Fawcett didn't have anything on her. Cheryl Tiegs, eat your heart out.

Bo Derek? Christie Brinkley? Not even close. My knees went weak the instant our eyes met across the busy hallway, and I experienced what could only be described as love at first sight. Her beauty crippled me like a sledgehammer struck out the wind. Her stare immobilized me, like a deer caught in headlights. Some people see angels in charred tortillas. I discovered an angel wearing lip gloss and Jordache pants.

I wasn't Casanova by any means. My enormous horse teeth and knobby knees didn't help me get a girlfriend, and I was extremely shy around the ladies, so the opposite sex showed me sympathy or charity, as they didn't regard me as a candidate for best hickey at the homecoming dance. Sure, I'd played spin the bottle at basement parties all over North Springfield, but I wasn't George Clooney. More like Barney Fife on a skateboard.

Nonetheless, I'd found my match, and I couldn't stop until I made Sandi mine. Every day, I'd rush home from school, shut my bedroom door, and write her poems and songs on my Sears Silvertone guitar, spewing my heart out to her in god-awful tunes that only she could hear. She had become my inspiration, my lighthouse, and every waking moment was spent daydreaming about our beautiful, inevitable union. I was hopelessly in love, and my skinny little heart couldn't bear another day without even a fragment of her reciprocation. Every day, I rehearsed my proposal to her in my head, and after what seemed like an endless period of painfully awkward courtship (handwritten notes passed between classes, phone calls after school... I laid it on pretty thick), I seized the opportunity and managed to turn on enough charm (and Old Spice) to ask her to be my girlfriend. To my surprise, she said yes (charity again), and we quickly progressed from simply walking side by side between classes to walking hand in sweat. I felt like a king. A Greek god. I, DAVID ERIC GROHL, WAS NOW OFFICIALLY COMMITTED TO A MUTUAL RELATIONSHIP WITH THE MOST BEAUTIFUL

GIRL IN THE WORLD—OR AT LEAST IN OUR GRADE. I had finally met my suburban soul mate, the love of my life, the one with whom I would grow old one day, surrounded by litters of adoring grandkids. I'd found my other half. And she'd discovered hers.

Or so I thought.

To be honest, I'm not sure if it lasted a week. I'm not exactly sure what happened. Things were going well for me! We were young, cheerful, and carefree! Siegfried and Roy are a power couple of epic proportions with limitless possibilities, similar to Burt Reynolds and Loni Anderson, David Copperfield and Claudia Schiffer. The world was our middle school oyster, and we had a lifetime of commitment ahead of us. And then, out of nowhere, she dropped the MOAB (Mother of All Bombs) on my ass.

"You know . . . I'm new here . . . and I don't really want to get tied down."

Such devastating sacrilege caught me completely off guard and stopped me in my tracks. Time stood still. My mind went blank. My throat constricted, and I couldn't breathe. My entire universe was wrenched from beneath my feet, and those words slashed through my heart like a poison scythe, knocking me down and reducing me to a puddle of anguish. I consented and smiled, but I was definitely dead inside. Annihilated.

Forlorn, I returned home to my volumes of nauseatingly romantic scribblings, gathered them together, and burnt them in a ceremonious ritual at the altar I had made in the carport for Sandi. Okay, maybe I just dumped them in the fucking trash can outside, but I did purge my pages of puppy-love poetry to break the figurative cord and move on with my dull teenaged life. I should have known she wouldn't love me. After all, I was simply a scrawny oddball who listened to bizarre music and wore tattered Toughskins that no one could comprehend.

Sandi and I grew apart over time. Different pals, different schools, various courses in life, finally losing contact and becoming only childhood memories for one another. In our twenties, I ran into her at a pub, and we laughed for a few minutes in a busy room, but that was it. The magic was gone. Again, we parted ways, returning to maturity and the persons we eventually became. Bygones, you know.

One day on the Foo Fighters' 2011 "Wasting Light" tour, a mutual buddy called and asked if I could add him to the guest list for our gig at the Verizon Center in downtown Washington, DC. It was my hometown's first sold-out arena, and my guest list was a virtual high school reunion, with over a hundred old friends attending the concert to rejoice and spend one night reminiscing about our distant past. It was almost as if I was going to attend the homecoming dance I had never been invited to! My pal graciously requested for a plus-one, adding, "Guess who's coming with me? Sandi!" Holy shit. I could not believe it. It had been nearly thirty years since we had met, and I had given her my heart, only for her to crush it into a thousand bloody pieces on the ground in front of me (please laugh), so I was overjoyed to have her join me and all of our old neighborhood friends. This was going to be a night to remember.

I must admit, I was a little nervous. Not for the show, of course (that was easy), but to see Sandi. It had been so long that I couldn't believe we would recognize each other after all of the twists and turns our lives had taken. What would she look like? What would she sound like? What would she wear? What would I wear? Hopefully, someone would graciously reintroduce us, and we'd go on with silly nostalgia all night until the house lights came on and we were obliged to pour out the champagne and go our own ways, back to the people we'd become. Suffocating with childish eagerness, I surveyed the busy backstage halls every few minutes to see if I could spot her before she noticed me, but she was nowhere to be found. After so many years, my teenage insecurity resurfaced. What if she declines the invitation? What if she doesn't want to see me? I didn't think my heart could take another heartbreak from Sandi. You're aware that even the oldest scars can reopen.

And then I saw her.

As she entered the dressing room, I stood up from my chair. It was like witnessing a ghost. I gave a gasp. I couldn't believe it: she looked precisely the same (except the Jordache pants and feathered hair, of course). Our gazes locked, and we both smiled as wide as the horizon before colliding in a long-overdue hug. The feeling now was obviously very different from the palpitations I'd felt by our lockers in the fluorescent-lit hallways of intermediate school, but there was a certain joy that you only get when you reunite with someone from your past, like a reassurance that life actually happened. We sat down and caught up for a while, talking about husbands, children, and relatives, laughing at the trouble we used to get into, and making a list of where all our old pals were now. The minutes flew fast, and it was soon time for me to get ready to play, so I asked Sandi to remain after the show for some more catching up over a beer or two. I dashed out the door to compose a set list while waiting for the house lights to dim.

The roar of the audience when we took the stage that night was the kind you can only hear at a hometown event. It was far louder than any previous gig on that tour, and it moved me to my core with emotion and pride. I grew up here, climbing trees, chewing tobacco, playing hooky, igniting fireworks, hunting creeks for crawfish, and spray-painting walls, so I was familiar with the streets and the people who lived there. I played each chord that night with all of my being to express my gratitude for a lifetime of Kodachrome memories, returning the tidal wave of love that flooded over me as we sang every song together. At one point, as I played a triumphant guitar solo from the stage's lip to a sea of screaming faces, blazing the fretboard to a rapturous response, I looked down and saw Sandi standing there... in the exact same spot where she had been standing in the dream I had the night my heart was broken. I stopped and realized that I had vividly visualized this same moment thirty years ago as a thirteen-year-old child, almost like a premonition, and now I was actually fucking living it! CRAZY AS IT MAY APPEAR, MY TEENAGE ROCK AND ROLL DREAM HAD COME TRUE. There was only one difference: Sandi wasn't sobbing excessively, filled with guilt that she had dumped me.

No.

Her ice-blue eyes shone as she uttered the iconic words, "Fuck you, asshole!"

THE SCARS ARE ON THE INSIDE

Slightly dizzy but painless, I gathered my strength, lifted myself up off the ground, and began walking the hundred and fifty yards back to my mother's doorway across the street. It was a lovely Saturday afternoon, and as it was on most weekends, our idyllic little suburban cul-de-sac was bustling with young people. Whether it was lawn mowers buzzing in the distance, bicycle bells chiming in time, or shouting kickball games in full flow, our neighborhood was filled with the sounds of happy youngsters playing outside. The kind of true-Americana stuff that spawned network television shows like The Brady Bunch and Happy Days. After all, North Springfield, Virginia, was purposely developed after WWII to have that appearance. House after small brick house, just big enough for baby boomers to raise a family of four on their paltry government salary, stretched for miles across a grid of groomed lawns, broken walkways, and tall white oak trees. Each morning, only a few minutes from the nation's capital, a long line of balding men in beige overcoats and briefcases waited to be carted off to the Pentagon or other faceless, monolithic federal buildings for another day at work. Life here was a consistent nine-to-five grind. A Groundhog Day rat race with only a gold watch at the finish line. For those misled by the "white picket fence" myth, this was a welcome reward of security and stability. For a lively, naughty child like myself, it was the devil's playground.

Saturday mornings would normally start with a bowl of cereal and a few cartoons before I glanced out the picture window in our living room onto the street to view the day's activities. If there was action to be found, I would quickly put on my Toughskins (cheap jeans from Sears that came in a rainbow of sickening hues) and leave with a high-pitched "Bye, Mom!" I will be back later!"I wasn't a recluse. I much preferred the countless adventures waiting to be found outside, such as crawling through dank drain pipes, jumping off rooftops, or throwing crab apples at unsuspecting cars from the bushes beside the road (an unwise prank that usually resulted in a frenzied high-speed chase, with me cutting through yards and hurdling chain-link fences with Olympic speed to avoid certain low-life retribution). From early dawn till the streetlights turned on, I would walk the pavement looking for thrills until I wore holes in my special sneakers, which had been modified with a raise on the left shoe to rectify my crooked spine.

On this particular day, however, I spotted my two best friends, Johnny and Tae, loading golf equipment into the trunk of their father's car. Golf? I thought to myself. We never play fucking golf. That's some bourgeois wealthy kid stuff. We had sticks. And it rocks! Crawfish-filled creeks! What did we need with our funny headgear and plaid trousers? I quickly suited up and skipped over to their driveway to investigate, only to discover that they had planned a family outing to the nearby golf course, leaving me to my own devices for the afternoon. As I waved goodbye in disappointment, I turned and walked back to my house, impatiently waiting for them to return by raking leaves and cleaning my room.

Hours passed slowly, until I spotted their blue Cadillac approaching the street. I instantly stopped what I was doing and went over to their house, where they were both swinging golf clubs madly at a practice ball on a string fixed into the ground like a tiny tetherball setup. Cool! As I got closer, I was in wonder as they chopped away at it like deranged lumberjacks, sending enormous pieces of soil and earth flying across the yard with each swipe. Having never attempted this new sport before, I carefully waited my turn, summoning every ounce of control my adolescent body could conjure until I was eventually handed the old, rusted club for my shot. This thing is heavy. ..I pondered as I raised my tiny arms to swing as hard as I could. Whiff. Miss. Whiff. Another missed opportunity. Giant chunks of sod flew in all directions like shrapnel, until I eventually connected, and with a beautiful ping, the ball spun in a circle around its post, giving me an amazing sense of accomplishment. My heart was flooded with pride. "It's my turn!"" Tae remarked, taking the club from my grasp and setting up the ball for another stroke. *I beat the crap out of that monster. ..I thought. You might want to double-check that the post is still firmly planted in the ground after all the pain I just inflicted on. ..I* leaned down and pushed the post into the soft dirt. ..WHACK.

If you've ever been hit in the head with a powerful blow, you'll recall the sound of impact as it resonates through your skull. It's a sensation that, like the bounce of a basketball or the thump of a less-than-ripe melon (as mine was), stays with you. And the silence that follows, usually accompanied by some lovely little stars and fairies, is deafening. I had just been clobbered full force by a teenager wielding an adult-weight pitching wedge designed for a "high-trajectory shot" on the course. With a nine-year-old boy's head, the consequence is quite different: Helter fucking Skelter.

Little did I know, my head had been split open like an overripe pumpkin long after the trick-or-treaters had left. I didn't feel anything. Zip. Nada. So, following Johnny and Tae's advice, I began my journey home, whistling uncomfortably and thought, *I'm in so much fucking trouble right now*, not recognizing the gravity of what had just happened. I was wearing my favorite T-shirt that day, a white ringer with the Superman "S" on the breast, and as I was crossing the street, I noticed the red and yellow emblem, but to my surprise, it was no longer my gorgeous Superman shirt. I was now enveloped in a sticky, coagulated mass of my own blood, scalp, and hair. I accelerated my pace in panic as I approached my yard, still feeling no pain but aware that one drop of blood on the living room carpet may bring this crisis to a head. As I climbed the few steps to the home, I could hear my mother vacuuming inside, so rather than barging through the door in a screaming, gory mass, I stood on the stoop and softly knocked, doing everything I could to calm the impending frenzy. "Mom? Could you just come here for a second?" I cooed in my calmest, sweetest "little boy who really fouled up this time" tone. "Hold on for a minute. .."She replied, ignorant to the terror that awaited outside, and finished vacuuming in the other room. "Umm, it's a bit of an emergency. .."I whimpered."

The sight of my poor mother's face as she rounded the corner to find her youngest child standing on the porch, drenched in his own blood, will stay with me forever. I felt her pain even if I didn't feel it myself.

Fortunately, my mother was not in attendance on June 12, 2015, at Gothenburg, Sweden's Ullevi stadium.

It was a stunning Scandinavian summer evening. Clear sky, a warm wind, and 50,000 Foo Fighters fans eagerly anticipating our tried-and-true two-and-a-half-hour, twenty-five-song setlist. At this point, our little band had progressed from arena to stadium level, becoming a tight, well-oiled machine that banged out song after song with little respite, and I was more than comfortable entertaining an audience of this size, living out my innermost Freddie Mercury fantasies on a nightly basis. Hearing a time-delayed full-throated sing-along ricocheting from the farthest rafters of a football stadium is an out-of-body experience, one that grows strangely addictive over time, reverberating in a chorus of beautiful connection. The open air hits you in gusts that give your hair a perfect Beyoncé blowout, as you absorb the smells of sweat and beer, which occasionally rises from the throng in a fog like condensation. The sound of fireworks above your head as you take your final bow and race to your dressing room, where a room-temperature pepperoni pizza awaits you. Believe me, it's everything you'd expect and more. I never completely embraced stadium rock until I experienced it from the stage's lip, and I've never taken a single moment for granted since. It is an unearthly sensation that can be summarized in two words: fucking awesome.

Before the show, a local promoter came into the dressing room to wish me luck and remind me that I had a lot to live up to, as the one and only Bruce Springsteen had previously played this stadium, and the audience was so enthralled that they "split the foundation" of the massive venue. There is no pressure! I never anticipated myself reaching to the level of "the Boss" himself, but I must admit, this pep talk turned up the heat a touch. I'm going to fuckin' give it to them good tonight, I thought, and resumed my pre-show routine, which normally included three Advils, three beers, and a room full of laughs. I confess that I have always been too embarrassed to perform traditional vocal warmups and exercises. Especially given that the majority of my performance consists of screaming bloody fucking murder rather than some beautiful, operatic coo. A few belly laughs and our version of "band prayer" (a non-religious moment in which we all take a shot of Crown Royal while staring into each other's eyes) always works.

The sun was still shining in the sky as we took the stage that night, and the crowd went wild as we opened with the first chords of "Everlong" (unquestionably our best-known song). This song, which we generally save for the finale, was the ideal choice to open what would become our most memorable show, and we plowed through it with the fervor of a band on fire. We jumped right into the fast-paced rock of "Monkey Wrench" as I sprinted from one side of the stage to the other, pounding my head and soloing like a kid with a tennis racket in his bedroom mirror. Stadium stages are not only broad but also incredibly high, allowing the crowd to watch the performers from hundreds of yards away, thus each movement is a fifty-yard dash, leaving you with little oxygen to sing the following line as you race back to the microphone.

Midway through the song, I lunged forward for another excursion to the wings (puns are my specialty), but my foot caught a cable that extended across the floor, causing me to stumble mere feet from the stage's edge. My body lurched forward, and I lost my footing as I looked down at the twelve-foot fall in front of me. No problem, I thought. I'll just jump. As I had done countless times from neighborhood roofs as a child, I put my best foot forward (see?) and hoped for the best. But this wasn't a rooftop overlooking a tidy suburban yard. No. This was harsh, unforgiving concrete with hard plastic walkways meant to protect the soccer field beneath it. My body smashed into the ground with a horrific BANG!, and a massive rush of terrified adrenaline surged in. How embarrassing! I thought. I quickly rose up and pretended it was just another small childhood tumble, but as soon as I took my first step, I realized something was wrong. When I put my weight on my right ankle, it felt warm and numb, like a sock full of mashed potatoes. It was just. ..mush. I collapsed to the ground again, clutching my leg as the local security personnel surrounded me. The band continued to play above my head, blissfully unaware of the tragedy happening beneath the high stage. I somehow attracted the attention of our band security guy, Ray, who was thirty yards away, and exclaimed, "I JUST BROKE MY FUCKING LEG!" Ray rushed to my aid, his enormous form rushing toward me as the band stopped playing and the song came to a standstill.

I requested a microphone and calmly proclaimed from the small lane of the steamy security pit, "Ladies and gentlemen, I believe I have broken my leg. I suppose I actually broke my leg. ."There was a stunned quiet in the stadium, as my loyal band looked down over the lip of the stage in bewilderment, watching as I was swiftly encircled by paramedics calling for a gurney. My thoughts raced as I tried to come up with something to say that would defuse or correct this ludicrous turn of events. Here I was, only two songs into a projected two-and-a-half-hour concert, about to be hauled off the field like an injured athlete in front of 50,000 people. These folks had come from far and wide, spending their hard-earned money to be entertained for the evening. I was going to give them a Boss-level performance, darn it. I thought, and then said the first thing that came to mind: "You have my promise right now, that the Foo Fighters. ..We'll come back and finish this show. .." I LOOKED UP AT OUR DRUMMER TAYLOR, MY BEST FRIEND AND PARTNER IN CRIME, AND SAID, "KEEP PLAYING!!!"

As I was brought to the side of the stage, the first notes of "Cold Day in the Sun," from our fifth album, boomed through the stadium, stunning the audience. A young Swedish doctor named Johan Sampson cut the laces of my high-top sneaker, and when he removed it, my foot dropped limp to one side. I had dislocated my ankle, shredding all of the ligaments that hold the joint together and breaking my fibula cleanly. He looked up at me and said, in his thick Swedish accent, "Your leg is probably broken, and your ankle is dislocated, so we must put it back in right now." My wife, Jordyn, and my tour manager, Gus Brandt, dashed to my side in horror, but all I could do was laugh at the absurdity of the situation. I told Gus to fetch me a tall Solo cup of Crown Royal and leaned over to my wife, grabbing the sleeve of her leather jacket and placing it between my teeth. "Go for it," I instructed the doctor, biting down on the salty black substance and feeling unusual pressure as they dragged my ankle back into place like an old key in a rusted lock.

"You'd better remain with me tonight. ..!!!Taylor sang. The Faces classic that we'd been playing for years rang in the background while another paramedic attempted to cover me with one of those Mount Everest Mylar blankets, assuming I was in shock. I can't really blame her. Perhaps I was. I was lying on my back, laughing, with a plastic cup filled to the full with whiskey, showing no evidence that I had just broken my leg in a big fall. At that moment, all I could think about was the duty of finishing the show for the thousands of people who had come to see us tear this building down with our well-oiled stadium-rock machine. I saw long lines of people heading for the exits, their hands falling low in disappointment, cursing our name and vowing never to see us again. I glanced at Johan, who was carefully holding my foot in place, and said, "Hi. ..Can I go up and continue the show while sitting in a chair?" "You'll need a brace." .."He told me. When I asked if they had one on hand, he told me that we would have to go to the hospital to get a brace placed, and then we could return. "How far is the hospital from here?""I spit back. "Thirty minutes," he responded. Fuck it! I thought. There was no way I was leaving this stadium without giving these fans what they paid for. "How about this? .."I explained. "You go to the hospital and get a brace, I'm going to sit down and play, and when you come back, we'll put it on." He stared at me in frustration and calmly warned me, "If I let go of your foot, it will fall back out of the socket!" Without hesitation, and in a moment of pure, stubborn will, I loudly exclaimed, "Well, you're coming up on stage with me, motherfucker!"

When I returned to my hotel in Norway that night, the pain had finally set in, and as I lay on the couch with my cast in the air, I couldn't help but remember those summer days I'd spent as a mischievous, hyperactive daredevil child, roaming the streets looking for thrills until I had holes in my sneakers, with no regard for the physical consequences. Only emotional consequences. And as I scrolled through the texts on my phone, I wept at the outpouring of love and concern from my friends after receiving the news. I knew what I needed to do.

YOU GET UP OFF THE GROUND AND WALK HOME. THE SHOW MUST GO ON.

JOHN BONHAM SÉANCE

The altar was set. Candles were lit. The ritual was prepared. I sat silently on the floor, facing the makeshift shrine I had built by hand from scrap wood and leftover model paint, cleared my mind, and began to pray. I'm not sure who I was praying to, but I know what I was praying for.

Success.

I sat quietly and meditated, hoping to open myself to the universe and receive divine intervention, imagining that every cell in my body would be transformed and empowered, bestowing upon me the supernatural abilities that my heroes must have possessed in order to transcend time and space through their music. There must have been some ethereal, magical aspect at work, I reasoned, and I was desperate to get into it, so I carried out my rudimentary ritual with the fierce, genuine conviction of a seventeen-year-old with nothing to lose.

The flickering candles at each corner of the board spilled their yellow light onto the cold concrete floor of my carport, illuminating the symbols I'd drawn to summon the spirits that would guide me to my destiny: the John Bonham three-circles logo and the number 606, two emblems with deep meaning in my life. I used my own brand of telepathy to list my deepest wants in the hopes that someone, somewhere, would hear my call and fulfill my prayers in due time. Manifestation was not a discipline I was very familiar with, but I believed that if you could perceive it, you could achieve it. This was my objective, with the universe's support.

Some refer to this as the "Law of Attraction," which holds that the universe creates for you whatever your mind focuses on. As a youngster, I understood nothing about this concept, but I believed from a young age that anything was possible if I put my mind to it.

At best, my alternatives in life were limited at this time. With no high school graduation and no family money, I was destined to live paycheck to paycheck, with music serving as my motivator, which was thankfully enough to keep my spirit alive. All I could do was dream. So, I dreamt. But I no longer dreamt about one day "making it" as a musician. I intended to subpoena the unknown to lead me there.

At a young age, I began playing the drums with my teeth, sliding my jaw back and forth and chomping up and down to replicate the sound of a drum set in my mouth, performing drum rolls and grace notes as if I were using my hands, without anybody noticing. Every morning, as I walked to school, I would hum melodies and perform drum parts with my teeth, playing my favorite songs and making creative compositions until I arrived at the front door and dumped my backpack into my locker. It was my best-kept secret, almost as if I was silently practicing drumming in my thoughts all day, teaching me new skills to try once I sat down at a real drum kit. During a childhood visit to the dentist, the doctor examined my sparkling whites, backed up, and inquired, "Do you chew a lot of ice?" Puzzled, I responded, "Ummmm... I don't think so?" He informed me that I had an exceptional degree of degradation from something wearing down my teeth, and I immediately recognized the cause. "I can play the drums with my teeth!" I proudly exclaimed. He looked at me as if I were crazy, so I told him to come closer, and he stooped down, placing his ear only inches from my mouth. I proceeded to perform Rush's "Tom Sawyer" for him, my jaw moving back and forth at lightning speed, the sound of calcium and enamel being chipped away like a tap dancer on a brittle stage, and his eyes widened as he stepped back in shock, telling me that I should reconsider this strange and orally harmful habit. However, there was no turning back. I was doomed with a lifetime of orthodontic percussion.

I've only met one other individual in my life who engaged in this unusual behavior: Kurt Cobain. It is particularly visible during our MTV Unplugged concert, which was recorded in New York City in November 1993. Kurt's jaw clenches and moves side to side at times during the show, acting as a metronome when he strums his guitar. This made great sense to me, because each musician produces his own unique "feel." Each artist follows an internal beat that is unique to them. As I stated in the foreword of Chad Kushins' John Bonham biography, Beast, this concept is difficult to articulate.

We all know that each musician plays differently, yet there must be something intangible that distinguishes the music written on a chart from what one drummer creates. Is it how each mind perceives a pattern? The internal clock that is determined by one's physical and mental makeup? How do they see the gap between the notes? I've seen numerous creators attempt to explain and manufacture "feel," but I believe that overthinking it is pointless. It is something holy that the cosmos alone can make, such as a heartbeat or a star. Each musician has a distinct design that is unique to them. I liken "feel" to the cadence of poetry; it can be comforting or upsetting, but it is always a gift from one soul to another. A romance between the giver and the receiver that serves to punctuate one's truth.

John Bonham's "feel" led me to that fateful night in front of my makeshift altar in the carport.

I had been listening to Led Zeppelin since I was a child, as their songs were always on rotation on the rock and roll stations of my youth, but it wasn't until I became a drummer that I realized the perplexing mystery of John Bonham's sound and fell head over heels in love with their entire catalog. When I listened to his drumming, I could hear voices calling to me, sometimes in whispers, sometimes in screams. This was something I'd never heard from any other drummer, and it almost scared me. Something about the gap between his notes caused my brain's electrical impulses to stutter, and time would slow in the milliseconds before each snare drum strike, as if I were plunging into a crushing black hole over and over. The weight behind his groove was more than physical; it was spiritual, and no matter how hard I attempted to replicate his playing, I understood it was pointless because this was more than drumming; it was his unique language exposed bare on vinyl.

Though he was technically impressive, I was more interested in why he played what he did. What was his intention? Why did his distinctive groove appear so much more natural than that of any other drummer, like an ocean tide slamming against towering cliffs and gently caressing the shore? What was it about his vibe that spoke to me? And did I have my own feelings? I eventually realized that this was the universe's work, and I would have to answer that question by offering myself up.

At this point in my life, I was interested in mysticism and the idea that a person could become one with God or the Absolute, so I was willing to investigate how that could happen (I was also interested in hallucinogens at the time), but I followed no specific credo in my selfish pursuit. And, while I knew the fundamentals of organized religion, I was not reared in a religious environment and only went to church with my Episcopalian father once a year on Christmas Eve, when we attended mass at DC's historic St. John's Church. I certainly connected with the spiritual component of it and found the ceremony to be beautiful and uplifting, but that specific set of beliefs had not been instilled in me from a young age, so everything remained a mystery to me. It wasn't until I was sent to a Catholic high school (for reform, not religion) that I learned about faith and started to understand what it meant.

Among my several Catholic religion classes, such as "Old Testament," "New Testament," and "Christian Scriptures," there was one that I particularly enjoyed: "Understanding Your Faith." This was more than just a list of psalms and verses to memorize; it was an investigation of the concept of faith, the unwavering confidence in something that transcends rationality and drives your life. Now that was something I could identify with, but in a very different environment. THERE WERE CERTAIN THINGS IN MY LIFE ON WHICH I RELIED UNCONDITIONALLY AND WITH UNWAVERING FAITH—MY MOTHER'S LOVE, MY LOVE FOR HER, AND THE LOVE THAT FILLED MY HEART WHEN I PLAYED MUSIC. So, without the typical structures and regulations, I thought of music as my religion, the record store as my church, rock stars as saints, and their songs as hymns.

As I sat in front of my punk rock tabernacle with its flickering lights, I reflected on that unconditional faith.

Was it witchcraft? I've been to a Wiccan ceremony and found it to be quite similar to my naive adolescent experiment all those years ago, but I can only call my tiny ceremony what it was to me at the time: an appeal to harness the power of the universe to achieve my ultimate goal. It's easy to dismiss it all as coincidence, but as I write this today, having tattooed both the three-circles logo and a gothic "606" into my skin, I have to believe that I manifested my destiny that night, whether through the Law of Attraction, calling upon the universe, tapping into a higher power, or whatever. I just know that the success I hoped for in my carport that night has finally arrived.

Or maybe I sold my soul for rock and roll?

PART 2

THE BUILDUP

YOU'D BETTER BE GOOD

"Okay . . . so, you wanna play some Zeppelin or AC/DC or something?"

Franz Stahl, the iconic guitarist of DC's greatest hardcore punk rock band Scream, was hunched over in a chair immediately in front of my drum set. As a seventeen-year-old mega-fan, I couldn't suppress my enthusiasm, nearly shaking on my drum stool while my callused hands held my broken drumsticks in white-knuckled anticipation, ready to jam with my personal idol. It was brutally evident that the strange feeling was not reciprocated. Franz appeared to be as excited about this audition as he would be about getting a double root canal at the dentist.

"No, man . . . let's do Scream songs!" I virtually yelled. He looked up from the guitar in his lap, slightly taken aback, and asked, "Oh yeah?" Which ones do you know?

This was the moment I'd been waiting for. I looked Franz directly in the eyes and replied, in my best Clint Eastwood-catchphrase tone, "I know them all..."

Soon, the gloomy, underlit basement of this Arlington, Virginia, head shop erupted in a deafening roar of wailing guitar and stratospheric BPM. Franz and I went through their whole catalog, album by album, even performing songs that hadn't yet been released to the public (okay, I did have a few bootlegs). With each song, I could see Franz's mood improve, as I required little to no guidance from any verse, chorus, or finale. He had no idea that his songs had been burnt into my memory. After all, except for one instruction from a local jazz drummer ("You're holding your sticks backward, David"), I'd essentially learned to play the drums by listening to Scream.

My punk rock baptism had happened only a few years before, and I had started collecting records with the fervor of a crackhead in heat, spending all of my hard-earned money on any album I could find in the hardcore section at Olsson's Books and Records in Georgetown, one of the few local record stores that actually carried underground music. Every penny of my Shakey's pizza and landscaping earnings went toward building a collection of loud, fast, and beautifully primitive albums that I would eagerly buy with crumpled bills and carefully counted coins, racing home to throw them on my turntable, inspecting every detail from the artwork to the credits as I played them on repeat at concert-level volume. My mother was an extremely tolerant woman who let me listen to whatever music I wanted (including the occasional Satanic death metal band).

However, screams were not the same. Their musicianship and dynamics were a little deeper and broader than most other hardcore bands, allowing them to easily transition between classic rock, metal, ska, and even reggae styles. More importantly, their songs were full of extremely appealing melodies that appeared to awaken the Beatles fan in me, whilst most other punk rock bands had to replace atonal cacophony due to a lack of creative ability. Furthermore, their drummer, Kent Stax, was a raw force of nature. He clearly knew more about the drums than most self-taught punk rock drummers, since his speed and technique were practically unrivaled. He looked like Buddy Rich in Doc Martens and a leather jacket, and you could tell he'd practiced his paradiddles.

With my pillows and a pair of huge marching band drumsticks, I would sit and play along to my Scream records till sweat practically dripped down my bedroom windows, trying my hardest to replicate Kent's lightning-fast drumming, which was no easy feat. I didn't have my own band at the time, let alone a drum set, but that didn't matter. I could close my eyes and envision myself as Scream's drummer, thrashing away to my favorite songs like they were my own.

Scream founded in 1979 after hearing the renowned Bad Brains play in a little venue downtown called Madam's Organ. They were a group of longtime friends who met in high school and went on to establish one of America's most iconic punk bands, and they were considerably older than me. Over time, they had become local heroes, admired by all musicians in the scene, and I would see them whenever I could. Lead singer Pete Stahl stalked the stage like a vagabond Jim Morrison, bassist Skeeter Thompson kept the grooves solid, and guitarists Franz Stahl and Harley Davidson (yep, you read that right) were a dazzling duo of crisp rhythms and solos. As morbid as it may sound, I used to fantasize about being in the audience at a Scream concert and hearing an announcement over the PA system that said, "We apologize for any inconvenience, but due to an emergency with their drummer, Scream will be unable to perform tonight." That is, unless there is someone in the audience who can step in for him.—and I'd jump up on the drum set to save the day. I realize it's juvenile, but hey—a kid can dream.

My skills as an amateur pillow percussionist went beyond the bounds of my ten-by-ten bedroom, and I began playing an actual drum kit in legitimate bands with names like Freak Baby, Mission Impossible, and Dain Bramage. My skills were rapidly improving, and I was putting all of the tricks I'd learned from jamming to my favorite songs into practice, eventually displaying my own bastardized versions of all my favorite drummers. Given my pillow-beating training, I was incredibly heavy-handed when I sat down behind a real drum set. I damaged skins and cymbals at an astounding and painfully expensive pace, to the point that I became a regular at the neighborhood music store, continually replacing my demolished gear while the jaded employees joyfully took my money week after week.

One day, as I passed the bulletin board full of flyers and advertisements on the wall by the front door of the music shop, I noticed a xeroxed sheet of paper out of the corner of my eye that read:

SCREAM LOOKING FOR DRUMMER. CALL FRANZ

I dashed home and hurriedly dialed the number from the phone on my mother's desk, ignoring the ungraded school papers. To my surprise, Franz responded, and after a stammering presentation of my fictional résumé (lies), he informed me that the band didn't have anywhere to practice right now, but he'd keep my number and contact me back when they could jam. I regarded it as a positive indication and waited for his response. Of course, I forgot to disclose a few essential details on the first call. The most obvious omission? My age. I couldn't believe he'd allow a seventeen-year-old high school junior without a car who still lived with his mother to audition for his band, so I did what any ambitious young rocker would do: I lied and said I was twenty-one.

When I arrived, I was greeted solely by Franz. With few to no expectations based on my dorky, plainly not twenty-one-year-old voice over the phone, I'm sure he notified the others that my audition was most likely a waste of their time and spared them the misery. My hopes for a one-night stand with the almighty Scream were quickly crushed, but that didn't stop me from playing like my life depended on it.

Because it did.

Franz was pleasantly surprised and asked if I wanted to come back and jam again sometime. I could not believe my ears. I had at least passed the first round. I cheerfully consented, painstakingly loaded my drum set back into the VW Bug, and went home with a heart full of pride, feeling as if I'd won the lottery.

The following audition was with the entire lineup. Apparently, Franz had told the band that I was worth listening to, and the others joined in, intrigued to see this thin, no-name guy from Springfield who knew every one of their songs beat the living shit out of his cheap Tama drum kit like he was playing in a stadium full of people. Now I was genuinely barking with the big dogs, surrounded by faces I'd only seen on album sleeves or in the audience, while dancing my heart out and singing out at the top of my voice. That dingy cellar was shaking with the magnificent sound of Scream, though Kent's rudimental drumming had been replaced with my unrelenting Neanderthal wallop, honed over years of racing in the sand.

After each successful rehearsal, I realized that my goal to jam with Scream for bragging rights was becoming more serious. They all agreed that I was the drummer they were looking for, so I was now presented with the real-life opportunity to join an established band that had made a name for itself with a killer catalog, a loyal following, and toured not only across the country but also internationally. My fantasy was coming true.

Now all I had to do was flip my life upside down.

Naturally, my mother was my primary concern. The woman who had given so much for me, devoted every moment of her life to my personal well-being, and showed me nothing but love since the day I was born. I never wanted to disappoint her since, in addition to being my mother, she was also my best friend. I could not let her down. I like to say that she disciplined me with freedom by letting me explore, discover my own way, and eventually find myself. I didn't want to jeopardize her trust, so I respected her and always kept my calm. I knew that leaving school at such a young age would shatter her heart, just as staying would break mine.

We sat at her desk, and with my head hanging in shame, I confessed that I intended to drop out of high school and travel the world. Her remark was

YOU'D BETTER BE GOOD.

I can only imagine that after twenty-five years of teaching underachievers like myself, my mother recognized I wasn't college material. But she had faith in me. She saw the light in me and realized that my heart, soul, and drive could not be learned from a chalkboard or a textbook under the mesmerizing hum of classroom lights. She would frequently say, "It is not usually the child that fails in school. Sometimes the school fails the student." So, like she always has, she allowed me the freedom to travel, find my own path, and discover myself.

My father had a different narrative.

My father and the guidance counselor read the riot act to me while I sat in the principal's office, flanked by my parents, and forecasted a most bleak existence of poverty and sorrow. I was a worthless punk in their views, a hoodlum rat with nothing to give other than filling their gas tanks on weekends or shining their loafers at the airport as they waited for their next flight, but I sat there like Rocky Balboa, thinking, Fuck you. I will prove you both incorrect. My favorite line? "You probably do all the things that a kid your age shouldn't do, like smoke cigarettes and drink coffee." Coffee? When was coffee classified as a class A drug? I proudly admitted to both.

As we proceeded to our respective cars in the parking lot, my father delivered one more punch before truly disowning me for good, screaming, "AND STAY OFF THE DRUGS!!!" It was the most quivering, Bob Dole-esque exhibition of tight-ass Republican wrath I'd ever witnessed, and it still is today. I could only laugh. His degradation could no longer harm me. I was finally free, and so was he. (I recall his driving a new, forest-green Plymouth Volare shortly after I graduated from high school, and I can only assume that the tiny college budget he had set up for me was promptly withdrawn and wasted on this most pimp-ass automobile). The cord had been cut, and I was free to bolt.

I BETTER BE GOOD, I THOUGHT.

After a few performances, we had crossed the Mississippi River, which was the farthest I had ever been from home, and I was getting used to this new life of truck stops and toll booths. To truly see America, you must travel it mile by mile, since you not only begin to understand the vastness of our lovely country, but you also notice how the climate and terrain change with each state line. These are things that cannot be learned from an old schoolbook under the cold classroom lights; they must be seen, heard, and felt in person to be truly appreciated. The education I was receiving on the road proved far more valuable to me than any algebra or biology test I had ever failed, because I was experiencing life firsthand and learning social and survival skills that I still use today.

Though I was finally free to pursue my lifetime ambition, I would periodically contact my mother to reassure her that she had made the correct decision by letting me go. Even hundreds of miles distant, I felt closer to her than anyone else and wanted her to know that the risk she had allowed me to take with my life was paying off.

Kansas City, Boulder, and Salt Lake City rushed by as we made our way to the West Coast, leaving a path of beer cans and burned stages in our wake. Within weeks, we were driving through the freezing rain and towering evergreens of the Pacific Northwest, on our way to Tacoma's Community World Theater, where we would perform with a young band called Diddly Squat. Great name, but an even better bass player, who I would meet years later to start our own band. Yes, Foo Fighters bassist Nate Mendel was a teenage punk like me, and our paths crossed a few times without official introduction, but that's how these things usually go; you just have to let the universe take the wheel. Thankfully, it did.

I have to admit that I didn't find the Pacific Northwest particularly intriguing at first. The suffocating covering of low-lying, gloomy clouds that permanently shut out the light in the fall seemed to sap both my energy and my attitude. Not to mention the "aroma of Tacoma," a scent emanating from the town's industrial paper mills, tinged with delicate undertones of boiling broccoli farts and dog feces, which drifted through the city depending on the direction of the wind. Lovely. I couldn't understand how anyone could live in such a dreary environment on a constant basis, but this was a part of the country I knew nothing about. One thing was certain: the cannabis was growing better with each mile further west.

My career as a dusk-to-dawn stoner was in full gear; I was smoking it when I had it and looking for it when I didn't. This was possibly life's toughest struggle on the road. Not only did you have to factor it into your $7.50 per diem (cigarettes, Taco Bell, pot), but you also have to have a good sense of party radar to know who was holding and who wasn't at all times. Jimmy and I were constantly on the lookout for any lanky metalheads with Slayer patches on the back of their leather jackets or crusty hippie-punks with dreadlocks tucked under a knit cap strolling around the venue. When we rarely scored, we would rush back to the van and scrutinize the marijuana, marveling at its superiority to the brown dirt stuff we were used to smoking back home, before getting as high as two Georgia pines right before the performance.

It was finally time to visit California, a place I never imagined I'd see. Standing in front of the Hollywood sign 2,670 miles from my small, lovely town made as much sense to me as raising a fucking flag on Pluto. Unfathomable. All I knew of America's most glamorized state was what I saw on television and in movies, so I envisioned all the cops to be from The Village People, all the kids from The Bad News Bears, and all the women from Charlie's Angels. (Turns out I was correct.)

With five days until the next event, we took our time driving down to Santa Cruz, a town I knew little about save that it was the setting for Corey Haim's vampire masterpiece The Lost Boys. Scream had been great friends with a Santa Cruz band named Bl'ast years before, and because almost everyone was part of this underground network group, they generously offered us a place to stay until our next gig in San Francisco. The eight hundred-mile drive was exhausting, but the scenery compensated for our claustrophobia. We wound through the mountain passes of the prehistoric Pacific Coast Ranges until we arrived at the Pacific Coast Highway, where we weaved between the mighty redwoods while giant waves crashed against the cliffs. I was in amazement. After watching the terrain transform into this natural beauty over long, grueling weeks and thousands of miles, I considered this the reward. I felt so lucky, alive, and free.

As we approached town, Pete stopped at a pay phone and called ahead to our host, Bl'ast pal Steve Isles, to give him an estimated arrival time. He returned to the van with great news: Steve's mother, Sherri, was preparing a delicious spaghetti dinner for us all, and we'd be staying at their gorgeous A-frame house just down the street from the beach for the next four days. This wasn't a tour anymore; it was Club Med. We grabbed Sherri a bouquet of flowers and a bottle of wine at the grocery store and hurried to our new digs, eager to escape the constraints of our van and feast like kings.

We were received like family, and before long, mountains of pasta were devoured, and fat joints of the most incredible marijuana I'd ever seen were passed around the table, the thick, delicious smoke rising in the air as we drank and shared road stories. To my surprise, even Sherri was smoking! Now, this was California. I thought my mother was cool. Sherri's generosity in taking in this wandering group of unkempt punk rockers, feeding them, smoking them out, and providing them with a warm place to sleep was nothing short of saintly. It was the most unselfish demonstration of hospitality I had ever witnessed. I fell asleep in my sleeping bag with a fuzzy smile and a full stomach.

Sherri was leaving town the next day, but she told us the leftovers were in the refrigerator and the cannabis was in the cabinet. Jimmy and I glanced at each other and dashed to the cupboard, where we discovered a giant mason jar filled with the kind of cannabis you'd only see in a High Times centerfold. We took a hairy, fluorescent-green bud and rode down to the beach on two Vespa-like scooters we found in the garage, where we discovered the Pacific Ocean. I strolled across the sand to the shore break, allowing the freezing water to run over my feet while I watched the sun sink behind the horizon. I'd made it. FROM ONE OCEAN TO THE NEXT, I CROSSED THE LAND ON NOTHING MORE THAN MY LOVE OF MUSIC AND MY WILL TO SURVIVE.

It surely couldn't get any better than this.

EVERY DAY IS A BLANK PAGE

"Has anyone seen Skeeter?"

A little hungover from another crazy night in Laurel Canyon, we all began to stir from our sleeping bags on the cramped living room floor of the old Hollywood bungalow that we had been sharing with a few Hollywood Tropicana mud wrestlers and took a head count. Pete, check. Franz, check. Barry, check. However, Skeeter was nowhere to be found. There was still time, I reasoned, because we didn't have to be at soundcheck for that night's gig until later in the day, so I crawled back into the comfort of my little cocoon for another few hours of sleep, closed my eyes, and crossed my fingers that, first and foremost, Skeeter was fine, but also that he hadn't abandoned us on tour thousands of miles from home with no money and no way back. Given his previous disappearances, this was a genuine concern.

By 1990, my travels with Scream had taken me from Louisiana to Ljubljana, Memphis to Milan, San Francisco to Stockholm, and I had become a seasoned road warrior, no stranger to the occasional crisis or conflict, so having one member missing in action was just another day on tour. What had previously been a crash education in how to exist on less than $10 per day in a van had become a familiar, comfortable routine, and I had readily adjusted to the life of a roving vagrant.

The European travels were especially thrilling; we visited locations I'd only seen on the nightly news or read about in my sadly neglected textbooks. But instead of the typical traditional tourist sites that most people visit when going abroad, I was discovering the globe through the sordid underbelly of the underground punk rock movement. Scream had previously visited Europe before I joined the band, so they had developed a network that welcomed us like family, providing us with somewhere to stay, food to eat, and equipment to use on tour because we couldn't afford to send our own instruments from home. Most of those pals were also musicians, and the majority of them lived in squats, abandoned buildings crowded with punks and anarchists, frequently stealing utilities from the city grid to make ends meet. These radical communities were not only intriguing to my young, impressionable mind, but also inspiring, as life in these makeshift communes was stripped down to its most basic human elements, foregoing the trappings of conventional existence (materialism, greed, and social status) in favor of a life of protest, freedom, and the realization that we all rely on one another to survive. I found it all pretty attractive, a far cry from the suburban white-picket-fence mindset I had left at home. The simple trade of a warm bed for a song laid the groundwork for my appreciation of becoming a musician, which I still rely on today and use to gain perspective when I feel lost in the tsunami of my now much more complicated life.

Amsterdam had become our home base for a variety of reasons, some obvious (marijuana), others purely logistical (proximity to northern Europe). We would usually save up our hard-earned money by working menial day jobs at home and flying standby on a Dutch airline called Martinair for $99 per person, arriving at Schiphol international airport, stealing a bike the first night, and spending the next few weeks preparing for our tour by making phone calls with a pirated phone card, gathering gear, and renting a van that would become our home for the next few months. To supplement our income, we would return bottles at the nightclub, gamble at the pubs, and even work odd jobs here and there. (I once worked at a small mail-order record company named Konkurrent, stuffing boxes full of albums to be shipped all over the world, just to support my weed habit until the tour started.) It was bare bones, but the hospitality and camaraderie shown to us by our gracious friends made us feel like we were living in the lap of luxury, and I eventually fell in love with the city so much that I even attempted to learn Dutch, a language I'm convinced is impossible to speak.

BUT, MORE THAN THAT, I WAS FREE, AND THERE WAS ADVENTURE AROUND EVERY CORNER.

One night in Amsterdam, as we were all drinking on the pavement in front of our favorite punk rock bar, De Muur, there was a sudden surge of energy across the street at the Vrankrijk, one of Holland's most notorious squats. An army of skinheads and right-wing fascists had planned an attack on the building, and as they marched up the short street, the people of the Vrankrijk braced for war. Blinding flood lights illuminated the balconies, and chicken wire draped over the windows as punks emerged from the squat with homemade weapons and shields. A full-fledged ruckus broke out, and we soon all joined in, tossing our beer glasses far into the air and raining them down on the mob of enraged fascists in explosions of smashed glass, like catapults firing warm malted bombs. Within minutes, the intruders surrendered and fled, and we went on with our night, now celebrating the uprising like Vikings returning from battle. This was not rock and roll. This was medieval stuff.

And that was only a Tuesday night.

Traveling across Europe's beautiful countryside became my favorite hobby, surpassing the lengthy, monotonous superhighways of our American excursions, but it also presented its own set of obstacles. As we moved from country to country, we encountered a new language every week, and communication was limited to a primitive kind of sign language that bordered on absurd miming. That being said, I was learning about languages and cultures that I would never have encountered in school, and the physicality of being in these places improved my sense of the world as a community, which is much smaller than most people believe. However, the border crossings were usually exciting. ..Imagine the excitement of a customs agent when a group of young punks arrives in a van with

Netherlands license plates (large red flag) with guitars and amps (bigger red flag). They would line us up on the pavement like criminals, tearing our van to shreds in search of any and all contraband. (I must admit, I've been subjected to more than a few body cavity searches over the years.) However, after watching the 1978 film Midnight Express one too many times, we were all responsible enough to know to smoke up all of our weed or hash before crossing any border, for fear of rotting away in a dark, dank prison. That being said, there was always a way to get around "the man." Whether it was stuffing our speaker cabinets full of Scream T-shirts to sell at shows (our bread and butter on the road) to avoid taxation from country to country or hiding small chunks of hash in Skeeter's dreadlocks so that we'd all have something to smoke on the long drives between shows (nothing like watching our bassist play with the drug dog at the border, knowing full well that his tangled mop However, there were some near calls along the way.

When I was going down an alleyway in Amsterdam with my old friend Marco Pisa, an Italian tattoo artist whom I had met in Bologna when I painted his tattoo shop in exchange for a beautiful branding on my left shoulder, we were approached by two junkies offering to sell us heroin. We weren't fans of heroin (or junkies), so Marco gently declined with a harsh "Fuck off!""We kept walking. They continued, following us closely, tapping our shoulders, and in an instant, Marco took out a switchblade with ninja speed and yelled, "FUCK OFF!"" Stunned, I turned to walk away, but in the corner of my eye, one of the junkies was going to smack me in the head with a metal pipe he had picked up from a work site we were passing by. Marco and I raced off like a shot, pursued by a swarm of shrieking zombies, just escaping before enjoying a delicious Thai lunch by the picturesque canals.

Even in the depths of my anguish and starvation, I never considered capitulation. What was I supposed to go back to? Begged my supervisor at the furniture warehouse to allow me return to ten-hour days of painting flamboyant sleeping sofas with deadly 3M chemicals. A lifetime of congested rush hour traffic, with strip malls and fast-food restaurants on every corner? I'd rather have been delirious in a cramped Spanish flat, shivering in a pool of my own sweat from a crippling flu as the roar of Barcelona's bustling Las Ramblas neighborhood boomed below. I'd rather have slept on a freezing nightclub stage in Linköping, Sweden, after the event, while paramedics raced in to save someone dying of a drug overdose. I'd rather have pulled in to play a squat in Italy, where they were burning their linens outdoors due to a scabies infestation, than have been cautioned not to eat the spaghetti served by a local promoter who was attempting to poison us in retaliation over a broken toilet.

"Ride or die," as they say.

However, it is possible that Skeeter abandoned us the first time due to our unstable lifestyle. On what would eventually be my final European tour with Scream, in the spring of 1990, he decided that, for whatever reason, he couldn't hang and returned home, leaving us stranded on another continent thousands of miles away. Fortunately, we had our good buddy Guy Pinhas fill in for a few performances, allowing us to complete the tour with just enough money to catch the standby flights back on El Al airlines, but I was beginning to suspect that Skeeter's commitment to the band was not the same as Pete's, Franz's, and mine. We would have done anything to prevent the wheels from falling off.

Though none of us were irreplaceable, the four of us had an undeniable chemistry, and Skeeter and I had a certain groove together, which he had instilled in me years before at one of our early rehearsals and was sorely missed when we played with a substitute bassist. When I first joined Scream, I was like a wild pony, playing as fast and as hard as I could while adding useless drum fills at the end of every line to dazzle everybody within earshot. Skeeter sat me down one day, rolled a gigantic joint from a tampon wrapper discovered in the toilet, and got me so high I couldn't see straight. "Okay, we're gonna play one riff, the same riff, for thirty minutes and you're not going to do one drumroll," he told me. Simple, I thought. I sat behind my kit as he began to play his silky bass line, which was half reggae and part Motown, and I confidently joined in. It wasn't forty-five seconds before I felt compelled to do a drumroll, but he shook his head and urged me not to, so I kept going with the beat. A minute later, I felt the unquenchable want to perform a crazy drumroll, almost like a type of musical Tourette's or holding back a sneeze, but Skeeter only shook his head. Skeeter was essentially breaking the wild pony, teaching me to value the simplicity and strength of a rhythm and to avoid unnecessary bravado. After 30 minutes, I was a completely different drummer. This was possibly the most valuable musical lesson of my life, and I will be eternally grateful to him for it.

The days passed, and thanks to the generosity of our mud-wrestling housemates, who returned home every night emptying their purses full of dollar bills into enormous piles on the living room carpet, we survived like strays. Food was sparse, and hunger quickly set in. Our roadie, Barry the Canadian, was having his Social Security payments shipped down to keep us from going hungry, but they only lasted so long. To this day, I will never use the phrase "doesn't amount to a can of beans," because I remember finding a can of beans in that kitchen and it literally saved my fucking life. Times were indeed difficult, but having been trained to face any hardship from years on the road, I did my best to keep my head up. It was not easy.

Night after night, I repeated this pattern, waking up in my sleeping bag on the living room floor with my eyes virtually swollen shut from the dust and grit of the canyon roads, returning to the reality of being a mud wrestler's stray pet.

And then I heard the five words that changed my life forever: "Have you heard of Nirvana?"

On a phone call with an old friend who grew up with the Nirvana guys in the little town of Aberdeen, Washington, I learned that they were between drummers at the time and had seen Scream perform just weeks earlier on our ill-fated tour. They were impressed with my playing, and I was given their phone numbers to call. Of course, I'd heard Nirvana. Their debut album, Bleach, was a watershed moment in the underground music industry, merging metal, punk, and Beatles-esque melody into an eleven-song masterpiece that would revolutionize the landscape of "alternative" music (while also costing $606). It rapidly became one of my favorites, distinguishing itself from all of the other noisy, heavy punk records in my collection by featuring SONGS. And the voice. ..Nobody has a voice like that. ..After a few more days of frustration and famine, I decided to take a chance and phone Nirvana's bassist, Krist, to inquire about the drummer position. Having never met him, I introduced myself and said that a common acquaintance had given me his phone number, so we talked for a bit until Krist informed me that the drummer post had already been filled by their good buddy Dan Peters from Mudhoney. It had been worth a shot, I reasoned, but it was not the end of the world. I gave Krist my Los Angeles phone number and told him to stay in touch and call me if they ever came down to L.A., as it was beginning to appear like the City of Angels was now my permanent domicile.

That night, the house phone rang. Krist called back. It seemed he had given the topic more attention. "Maybe you should talk to Kurt," he said. Danny Peters, while an incredible drummer in his own right, had a totally different approach than mine, playing with a more sixties rudimental feel as opposed to my basic, Neanderthal disco dynamic, which seemed to be more Nirvana-friendly. Krist and Kurt also felt horrible for stealing Danny from Mudhoney, one of their all-time favorite bands. So I immediately called Kurt, and we spoke about music for a long time. From NWA to Neil Young, Black Flag to the Beatles, the Cramps to Creedence Clearwater Revival, we discovered that we had a lot of musical similarities and that an audition might be worthwhile. "Well, if you can make it up here, just let us know," he casually replied in a drawl that the world now recognizes. We said our goodbyes, and I was presented with one of my most difficult decisions.

I'd felt like a part of the Scream family since the day I first joined. Even though I was considerably younger than Pete, Franz, and Skeeter, they always treated me as an equal, and we became best friends, spending nearly every day together, tour or no tour. I had spent the most important, formative years of my life with them, discovering music, the world, and, ultimately, myself, so leaving them behind on that sinking ship hurt my heart in ways I had never felt before, even more than saying goodbye to my own father when he disowned me for dropping out of high school. We had always been in this together, all for one and one for all, and we had overcome so much adversity. However, the severity of this new issue made me reconsider my future. So, whenever I was unsure about my future or needed a voice of reason or wisdom, I phoned the one person who had never steered me wrong in my life. ..My Mother.

On a collect call from the parking lot of an Orange County record store, I tearfully recounted my situation, and she completely understood since she felt the same way I did about Pete and Franz. We had all formed a family over the years, and she saw them as more than just bandmates; they were my brothers. To this day, I will never forget the sound of her voice giving me the guidance that guided my life to its ultimate destination.

"I'm David. ..I know you care about your pals, but sometimes you have to put your own needs ahead of others'. You must take care of yourself." Coming from a lady whose entire life had been the polar opposite, this utterly astonished me, but because she was the wisest person I knew, I hung up the phone and resolved to follow her advice, regardless of the consequences.

I put my duffel bag, sleeping bag, and drum kit into a cardboard moving box and drove up to Seattle, a town I'd only been to once and knew almost no one, leaving one life behind to begin another. I felt a loss like I had never known before. I missed my home. I missed my friends. I missed my family. I was now completely on my own, beginning over. However, I was still hungry. And, never one to let my wheels spin, I had to keep moving. After all, I was still free, and adventure awaited around every corner.

BECAUSE EVERY DAY IS STILL A BLANK PAGE, WAITING TO WRITE ITSELF.

IT'S A FOREVER THING

"Do you mind if we take a break? I've never done a tribal tattoo before."

Believe me, these are not the words you want to hear as a man drills a thousand times per second into your skin with a needle full of black ink as you desperately attempt to bear the blistering pain of being forever branded while crying like a baby. But the beads of sweat streaming down his forehead and his squinting red eyes were definitely not a good sign, so I got up from my chair and went outside for a little smoke after a quick and painful wipe with a paper towel. The complicated pattern I had personally sketched (based on the original John Bonham "three circles" emblem) had to be razor sharp, with straight, even lines and flawless circles linked to form a piece that would wrap around my right wrist like a threatening Celtic bracelet. Even for a seasoned professional, this was a difficult undertaking, and his weary frustration was far from comforting. Nonetheless, it had to be correct, and there was no going back.

After all, it's a permanent thing.

It was the fall of 1990 in Olympia, Washington, and I had just received my first check as a paid Nirvana member. It was the largest payday of my professional life up to that moment, totaling $400. This much-needed advance from our newly acquired management business, Gold Mountain, came at a time when Nirvana was being courted by every major-label record company in the world in an all-out bidding war, while Kurt and I were virtually hungry and living in squalor. Our apartment at 114 NE Pear Street was the back unit of a decaying old home built about 1914, with one bedroom, one bathroom, a small living room, and a kitchen the size of a broom closet (ironically, right across the street from the Washington State lottery headquarters). Versailles was not. "Unclean" doesn't begin to convey the devastation inside. It turned the Chelsea Hotel into a Four

Seasons. Whitney Houston's restroom was turned upside down. A trailer-park tornado left behind ashtrays and magazines. Most people wouldn't dare to enter such a dangerous cave, but it was our humble abode, and we considered it home. Kurt slept in the bedroom, while I slept in my sleeping bag on an old brown couch covered with cigarette burns that was way too small for my six-foot frame. At the end of the couch was an old table where Kurt kept a pet turtle in a filthy terrarium. Kurt, a true animal lover, had an odd, perhaps metaphorical, admiration for turtles because their shells, which provided the most protection, were actually incredibly sensitive. "Like having your spine on the outside of your body," he once explained. But, as lovely and anatomically poetic as that feeling was, it soon made no difference to me, because this goddamned reptile kept me awake every night by hammering its head against the glass for hours on end in an attempt to escape our shared home of filth. I couldn't blame the poor thing. I often felt the same way.

At the time, I had worked out how to get a three-for-ninety-nine cent corn dog special from the Ampm petrol station across the street. The trick was to eat one for breakfast (at noon) and save the other two for a late dinner after rehearsal, which kept me going until the hunger pangs returned and I was forced to shamefully return to the fluorescent glow of the convenience store lights, clutching another crumpled dollar bill. (To this day, I tremble when I see a battered frank skewered on a pointed wooden stick.) It was just enough fuel to keep my twenty-one-year-old metabolism going, but it provided no significant nutritional value. This impoverished diet, along with my desire to play the drums five evenings a week with every fiber of my thin existence, had reduced me to a virtual waiflike marionette, barely filling out the soiled old clothes that I kept in a duffel bag on the floor in the corner of the living room. It was enough to drive anyone back to the comforts of their mother's cooking with their tail between their legs, but I was 2,786 miles away from Springfield, Virginia. And I was free.

Our evenings in Olympia quickly became spent shooting cartons of eggs from a distance in the backyard of our old house and playing Super Mario World until the sun came up. Our filthy cave had suddenly been turned into an adolescent amusement center from hell. For me, this was Versailles. However, because I had neither foresight or care for realistic spending, the money quickly decreased, leaving me with just enough cash for one final crazy indulgence: a tattoo. Not my first, mind you. No, that was a self-inflicted artwork that I created with a sewing needle, thread, and a container of black ink when I was fourteen years old. After viewing the gritty homemade-tattoo sequence in Uli Edel's cinematic masterpiece Christiane F., I decided to bedazzle my left forearm with the insignia of my favorite band at the time, Black Flag. After gathering all of the required components from the dusty junk drawers throughout the home, I waited until everyone was asleep before erecting a makeshift tattoo studio in my bedroom and beginning my devious operation. I sterilized the sewing needle with a candle flame, gently wound the thin thread around the tip, and dipped it into the container of ink, watching the fibers absorb the thick black liquid. Then I began, using a steady hand. Poke, poke, poke. The sting of the needle as it punctured my skin sent shivers down my spine, and I paused every now and then to wipe away the excess muddled pigment and assess the damage. Kat Von D I was not, but I persisted, inserting the needle as deeply as my pain tolerance would allow to assure that this profound image would never fade. If you've seen the renowned Black Flag logo, you'll recognize it as four thick, black vertical bars arranged in staggered sequence. A tall order for a neglected teen with his mother's seldom-used sewing gear. I managed to go through three of the four bars before saying, "Fuuuuck this shit!" and pausing. Not the pièce de résistance I had hoped for, but my heart was filled with a sense of finality that energized me. Something that exists indefinitely.

As the years passed, I had quite a collection of these small fuzzy diaries all over my body. A little mark here, a little mark there, until I was ultimately given the opportunity to get legally tattooed by an Italian artist named Andrea Ganora, who resided in a notorious squat in Amsterdam called Van Hall. In late 1987, a small gang of punk rockers from all over Europe took over an ancient two-story factory and occupied it. Dutch, Germans, Italians—it was a close-knit group of friends who transformed the frigid, cavernous structure into their home, complete with a live music venue downstairs (where I also recorded my first live record, SCREAM Live! at Van Hall, in 1988). When I was 18 years old, it became Scream's virtual home base. Andrea was the resident tattoo artist, and the majority of Van Hall's inmates proudly displayed his work. He was a true artist, but unlike the clean, laboratory-like environment of most licensed tattoo shops, his studio was his bedroom, and his tattoo gun was fashioned from an old doorbell machine. We smoked joint after joint while listening to punk and metal music, with our laughter and the electric buzz of his tattoo gun filling the room. To this day, I can vividly recall the pleasure of my first "real" tattoo, as well as his strong Italian accent and the wonderful smell of hash, every time I look in the mirror at the present he gave me that evening. Thirty-three years later, the hue has yet to fade.

My Lifestyles of the Rich and Famous honeymoon on Pear Street was soon over, and I was back to rationing corn dogs and dreading the turtle terrarium's constant tapping, head buried in the soiled cushions of that old couch. I've learned my lesson. The season got dark, and homesickness struck in. I'd left my friends, my family, and my beloved Virginia behind for... this. The harsh Pacific Northwest winter weather and lack of sunlight only exacerbated the sense of despair lurking in the shadows, but thankfully, I still had one thing stopping me from returning home: music. As dysfunctional as Nirvana could be at times, there was an underlying focus once we plugged in our instruments and the amps started to shine. We wanted to be great. Or, as Kurt once told music entrepreneur and giant

Donnie Ienner during a courtship in his New York City high-rise office, "We want to be the biggest band in the world." (I assumed he was kidding.) Our rehearsal space was a barn-like structure turned into a demo studio, located thirty minutes north of Olympia in a Tacoma suburb. It was one little step above an old, damp basement, but it had heat and a small PA system (as well as some iffy shag carpeting), so it met our basic needs. Kurt and I would make the trip five days a week in a Datsun B210 that had been handed to him by an elderly woman, barely making it up Interstate 5 without the wheels falling apart (one did once, lug nuts scattered across the gravel road in the dark). Our music was the one thing that kept my mind off the flaws of this new life I had taken on, the one thing that made everything worthwhile. Every rehearsal began with a "noise jam," which evolved into a sort of improvisational dynamics exercise, eventually honing our collective instinct and allowing song structure to happen without being verbally arranged, almost like a flock of blackbirds gracefully ebbing and flowing in a hypnotic wave over a country field in the winter. This strategy contributed to the quiet/loud dynamic for which we became recognized, despite the fact that we did not originate it. That credit goes to our heroes, the Pixies, who were extremely important to us. We'd incorporated their simple hallmark into a number of our new songs: tight, concise verses that explode into massive, shouting choruses. A sonic juxtaposition with fierce results, particularly "Smells Like Teen Spirit."

As the long winter gave way to spring, we spent many hours in that makeshift studio working on songs for what would eventually become the album Nevermind. Unlike previous bands I had been in, Nirvana did not play shows frequently for fear of exhausting the local audience, so the majority of our attention was focused on being ready to record once we had chosen a label and producer. Kurt was incredibly prolific, appearing to have a new song concept virtually every week, so there was always a sense of forward motion, never feeling trapped or stagnant musically. After he closed his bedroom door at night, I would hear the calm strumming of a guitar from his room and sit on my dirty old couch, waiting for his light to go out. Every day, I couldn't wait to find out whether he had anything new after we arrived at practice and hooked in. Whether he was making music or entries in his now-famous notebooks, he had an incredible need to create, despite the fact that he kept it a secret. His songs might surprise you. And they were never introduced with, "Hey, I wrote something great!" They would just materialize.

When I joined Nirvana in September 1990, the band had already produced a fresh batch of songs with their previous drummer, Chad Channing, that were slated for their next Sub Pop LP. Songs such as "In Bloom," "Imodium" (which became "Breed"), "Lithium," and "Polly" were recorded earlier that year by Butch Vig, a young, up-and-coming producer from Madison, Wisconsin. These songs demonstrated Kurt's ever-evolving songwriting abilities, with a new, mature sense of melody and lyric; they had outgrown the prior material and promised great things to come. Simply put, Nirvana was becoming Nirvana. Paired with Butch's mega-fucking-rock sound, this album was responsible for the majority of the industry "buzz" surrounding the band, eventually sparking an ongoing feeding frenzy of interest. These songs would have been an embarrassment of riches for most bands to rely on, but Kurt kept writing and new songs kept coming. "Come As You Are," "Drain You," "On a Plain," "Territorial Pissings," and last but not least "Smells Like Teen Spirit." Usually starting with a riff from Kurt, Krist Novoselic and I would follow his lead with our seasoned intuition, acting as the engine room for his screaming vision. Hell, my job was easy! I could always tell when a chorus was coming by watching Kurt's dirty Converse sneaker move closer and closer to the distortion pedal, and just before he pressed the button, I would blast into a single-stroke snare roll with all of my might, like a fuse burning fast into the heart of a bomb, signaling the change. The resulting eruption would frequently send shivers up my spine, as the sheer power of our collective sound grew almost too large for that small place. These songs wouldn't stay a secret for long. They would soon sneak up on everyone and take the world by surprise.

WE WERE SURROUNDED AND THERE WAS NO WAY OUT

WE WERE SURROUNDED. AND THERE WAS NO WAY OUT.

Welcome to the fall of 1991.

Trees nightclub in the Deep Ellum section of downtown Dallas, Texas, was just another stop on the North American part of our "Nevermind" tour, which had a tight schedule of thirty rigorous gigs in forty days. With a maximum capacity of approximately 600 people, this relatively new club was identical to the majority of the other venues planned for that tour: crowded, a low stage, minimal PA and lighting, and a small dressing room in the back to prepare for (and recuperate from) another cathartic performance. As intimate as Trees may appear in retrospect, it was actually one of the larger rooms booked for us on that trip, as we were more accustomed to playing much smaller venues like the Moon in New Haven, Connecticut, where we had squeezed 100 people into its tiny, low-ceilinged room just a few weeks before, or J.C. Dobbs in Philadelphia, which was sold out with 125 paying guests a few days later, or the 9:30 Club in Washington, where we undoubtedly exceeded their declared capacity of 199 a few days later. Nirvana was no stranger to a Saturday night sweatbox, so the sudden transition to much larger, 600- to 1,000-capacity venues like the Masquerade in Atlanta, St. Andrews Hall in Detroit, and now Trees in Dallas felt like slipping on Andre the Giant's tighty-whities: a little roomy around the sensitive bits.

Traveling in our newly rented passenger van with a trailer full of gear hitched behind, the band and three crew members spent most days driving, reading, listening to music, and attempting to catch a quick nap on our crowded bench seats, exhausted from the night before. Fortunately, this time there were hotel rooms along the route.

Thank God. A luxurious upgrade from my days in Scream, where we either slept in the van, crashed at the house of some random stranger we met at the gig, or sometimes resorted to laying out our sleeping bags on the beer-soaked stage we had just rocked hours before for a good night's sleep (yes, I have cuddled up to my drum set on multiple occasions). There was also a significant wage increase. In fact, it is double! The increase from my $7.50-a-day Scream per diem to Nirvana's $15 made me feel wealthy beyond my wildest imagination. I wasn't quite ready to put down a deposit on a Hamptons mansion just yet, but I had finally progressed from generic cigarettes to authentic Marlboros, which made me feel like a fucking king. At twenty-two years old, I had finally attained a long-awaited milestone in my life: touring the world comfortably with a band that was selling out shows to amazing reviews and quickly gaining recognition. However, this may have happened too soon.

Nirvana's Nevermind was released on September 24, 1991, just a few days after the first show of the tour, and within a week, I noticed a difference. Not only did we pull large numbers to the events, but also different types of crowds. They were no longer made up of Sub Pop fans and college radio junkies eager to hear their favorite songs from the band's debut album, Bleach; there was an unexpected flood of folks who appeared to be more. ..mainstream. The customary attire of Salvation Army flannels and Doc Martens was replaced with designer jeans and sports shirts, similar to what suburban youth in Springfield wore. The "Smells Like Teen Spirit" single, released two weeks before the album, swiftly spread outside our home zone and into the hands of a far larger audience, enticing more and more people to come see what all the commotion was about. The audience was expanding rapidly. There were often more people outside than inside the venues. THE SECRET WAS OUT.

I felt a tug of battle inside. As a child, I had discovered rock and roll on the AM radio in my mother's car, singing along to 1970s Top 40 songs, but I was now torn about the prospect of having a Top 40 hit myself. All of those years as a "punk rocker," renouncing mainstream music and yelling "sellout" to any band that moved even marginally toward mainstream success, had twisted my music-loving heart into a confused and callused lump within my jaded chest. I had become cynical and judgmental, frequently unsure what was acceptable to "like" or "dislike" based on the standards of cool culture in the punk scene. However, I was also pleased that an increasing number of people were turning out to share the music I adored and took great pride in creating and performing. It was a moral quandary that would be both motivating and damaging to the band.

Kurt found this crossroads even more distressing than I did. The same guy who had yelled, "We want to be the biggest band in the world," to a record company executive in a New York City high-rise office was now faced with the terrifying prospect of that being a reality. Of course, we never expected the world to change for us (since we were never going to change for it), but with each passing day, it seemed more and more likely. And it was overpowering. Even the most stable can break under such pressure.

One issue was that we were now attracting the same folks who used to bully us in high school for being different, calling us "faggots" and "queers" because of the clothes we wore and the music we listened to. Our fanbase shifted to include macho monster-truck homophobes and meathead jocks whose lives revolved around beer and football. We'd always been the misfits. We had always been the oddballs. We weren't one of them. So, how do they become one of us?

Then the footage came out.

On September 29, only a few days after the release of our album, the "Smells Like Teen Spirit" video premiered on MTV's 120 Minutes. 120 Minutes, a late-night alternative music program, was credited with launching the careers of numerous underground bands, including the Pixies, Sonic Youth, Dinosaur Jr., and Hüsker Dü. It was an incredible honor for a band like ours to be featured in such esteemed company. It was a watershed moment, not only personally but professionally, and to deny that we were overjoyed would be a lie. On a night off between our gigs in New York City and Pittsburgh, we sat in our hotel rooms, waiting for our film to be screened for the first time. Kurt and I shared a room on that tour, and I remember laying across from each other in our twin beds with the television turned on, watching movies from Morrissey, the Wonder Stuff, and Transvision Vamp for what seemed like an eternity; the suspense was painful with each passing second. The Damned, Red Hot Chili Peppers, and Nine Inch Nails, video after video, until. ..There we were! First, we taped a little promo backstage at the Reading Festival in England a month ago, where we awkwardly exclaimed, "You're watching 120 Minutes!"" from the food tent behind the stage, Kurt's arm still bandaged in a sling from his manic dive into my drum kit that day. I yelled from my stiff Best Western bed, feeling both ecstatic and like I was on acid. Holy stuff! I thought. Is that what we look like? And suddenly, without more ado, the familiar chords that had once resonated through our dismal little rehearsal space in Tacoma rang through the dresser's tiny Magnavox speakers. It was really happening. I was watching MYSELF on MTV. Not Michael Jackson, or the Cars. Not Madonna, or Bruce Springsteen. No. Krist, Kurt, and I were performing a song we wrote in a filthy barn. This scene was more weird than Dalí's melting clocks ever were.

We excitedly took up the bedside phone and called room after room, exclaiming, "It's on!" It's currently on!" Like kids at a slumber party, the poor hotel operator kept pinging us back and forth to busy signal after busy signal. This was a moment I'll never forget, filled with amazement, celebration, and shock. From the dirty maroon carpet to the chipped wooden furniture, if I close my eyes today, I can vividly recall every detail, because this was an event that altered not just my life, but the world of music at the time.

This video contributed to the impending tsunami. Inspired by Jonathan Kaplan's 1979 film Over the Edge, starring Matt Dillon, the "Teen Spirit" video was a dark depiction of teenage revolt, recorded with actual fans from a gig we'd performed the night before at the Roxy in Hollywood. Kurt and filmmaker Samuel Bayer imagined a high school pep celebration turned riot, with disgruntled youths, tattooed cheerleaders, and young punks destroying the gymnasium in a euphoric mosh pit, leaving their angst and despair in a blazing mound of debris and ash. This was a sentiment that we were all obviously connected to—but we couldn't have predicted that an entire generation would feel the same way. Initially, the tape was only broadcast at night because MTV deemed it too controversial for prime-time viewing, but it quickly made its way into the regular rotation. Once there, it spread like wildfire, destroying our entire planet.

Nirvana was quickly becoming a household name. In just a few weeks, the band's hype had reached fever pitch, with all eyes on the fuzzy enigma of three scruffy freaks in their early twenties, equipped with tunes that your cool aunt and uncle could sing along to. Surprisingly, the world inside our stinky small rental van hadn't altered much: duffel bags and cassette cassettes, fast-food cartons and discarded cigarette packets. Typical of a band like us. The world outside of our tiny bubble was rapidly changing: autographs and radio interviews, packed arenas, and repeated near-riots. We had to abandon the stage at our Mississippi Nights show in St. Louis just days before our show at Trees due to the crowd rushing the stage, prompted by Kurt's frustrations with the local security being too rough with the fans, a common occurrence for venues unfamiliar with slam dancing and stage diving. It was complete anarchy. At the time, I was using borrowed drum equipment from our opening band,

Urge Overkill, after Kurt and I shattered mine to splinters in Chicago. As waves of kids poured over the barrier onto the little stage, snatching our equipment and yelling into the microphones, I returned to Urge Overkill's dressing area and joyously exclaimed, "There's a fucking riot going on out there!" to which the drummer, Blackie, replied, "Shit! My drums!"

By the time we got to Dallas, we had no idea what to expect. But there was a special electricity in the air that night, exacerbated by abnormally swampy humidity, which added to the tension in the room, like a short fuse on a homemade bomb. As soon as we came onstage to play, the crowd was spilling over the floor monitors and onto Kurt's and Krist's guitar pedals, and the band hadn't even started playing. Imagine yourself pushed up against a wall by a crowd of six hundred alcohol-fueled adrenaline junkies ready to tear you and the entire place apart; increase that by 10, and you'll have a sense of what it was like to be in Nirvana that night. To make matters worse, we had technological difficulties immediately. So, while we waited for our equipment to operate correctly, we stood there snarkily playing a horrible version of "L'amour est un oiseau rebelle" while our guitar techNic Close hurriedly sprinted from one side of the stage to the other, doing his best to salvage this possibly hopeless scenario. Kurt said a few things, then we started with the first song, "Jesus Don't Want Me for a Sunbeam," a rendition of one of our favorite Scottish bands, the Vaselines.

The venue went insane, as the audience's manic, raw energy increased exponentially minute after minute. By the time we got to "School," six songs into the set, the crowds on stage had become so dangerous that Kurt couldn't sing into the microphone without getting kicked in the face and crashing into his teeth. I could sense Kurt's aggravation, and I knew exactly what happened when he became irritated. Something was about to be destroyed, whether it was his guitar, his amplifier, or my drums. I knew it was going to happen. The countdown began. ..Four songs later, following a raucous, technically challenging version of our generally beautiful acoustic tune "Polly," Kurt snapped. Turning to his left, he ripped off his guitar and began hacking the monitor engineer's soundboard to bits, sending buttons, knobs, and shrapnel flying over the stage. Kurt had enough. Not just of this show, but of everything that had brought us here tonight. Kurt's fury had finally boiled over after weeks and weeks of increased chaos, and he was now releasing it in a ferocious display of violence. The audience clapped, delighted, as if this were some kind of performance. If only they knew. This wasn't an act. This was real.

Nonetheless, we soldiered on, playing while the monitor engineer jokingly placed a wood pallet over his mixing desk, fearing further thrashing. Nothing could help him now. This speeding train had already gone off the rails, colliding with everyone and everything in its path. We launched into another cover, Shocking Blue's "Love Buzz" (Nirvana's debut song), and the craziness continued. Body after body fell to the stage, the room heating up with each distorted chord, every inch of skin soaked with the sweat of six hundred strangers. After the song's second chorus, Kurt plunged into the throng, guitar in hand, and soloed while crowd-surfing atop the gyrating mass of greasy hair and tattooed legs. As he tumbled back to the stage, flailing in a frenzied, spasmodic dance, he landed on a massive security guard who had been stationed there to keep the children offstage. Attempting to push Kurt away, he used brute force on Kurt's small frame, and in a fight-or-flight moment of instant, defensive reaction, Kurt smashed the body of his guitar into the security guard's head, tearing open his flesh and drawing streams of blood that immediately began pouring down his sinister Mohawk. Kurt was taken aback when he realized he'd been cut, and as he rose up, the enormous security guard hit him right in the jaw, knocking him to the floor. Krist and I immediately dropped our guitars and intervened to save our comrade as the song came to a sudden, crashing halt. Krist attempted to negotiate with the security guard, even removing his own shirt to assist stop the bleeding amid screams of "BULLSHIT!" BULLSHIT! BULLSHIT!" echoed through the clubhouse. Kurt went out to the opposite side of the stage in a trance as I made my way to the exit, convinced that it was all over.

It was not.

After some pleading from a club staffer who feared an impending riot, we opted to finish our show while the stage was still soaked with blood. Kurt's guitar was severely out of tune due to the blow he had administered to the security guard's cranium, but that had never stopped us. The harsh, detuned sound almost heightened the unpleasant atmosphere in the room. After finishing the concert with our quickest, most punk-rock-sounding song, "Territorial Pissings," we eventually laid our instruments down and proceeded to the dressing room, rather frightened by the evening's unusual turn of events. We were used to commotion and disarray, but this was different. This wasn't fun. This was dark. At least it was done.

We all made it through another day, and our traveling circus continued on to the next city. With twelve days remaining on the journey, there was still time for the wheels to fall off, but at least we were on the correct track: home.

We were completely exhausted when we returned to Seattle for a final homecoming gig on Halloween. We had left our mark and returned with the scars to show it. In just forty days, we had transformed from three disheveled young men with little to lose to three disheveled young men with a gold record. Our worlds had changed forever, as had yours.

WE WERE SURROUNDED. AND THERE WAS NO WAY OUT.

PART 3

THE MOMENT

HE'S GONE

"He's gone, Dave."

On March 3, 1994, I awoke in Seattle to learn that Kurt had overdosed in a hotel room in Rome. I quickly switched on the TV and saw images of him strapped to a gurney as he was carried to the hospital in an ambulance, so I anxiously called everyone on our team to find out what was going on, hoping that it was simply another accidental overdose, as it had occurred before. There was chaos and conflicting reports; some were depressing, some encouraging, but no matter how badly I wanted to be there, I was five thousand miles away and completely impotent. After all, I had just seen Kurt two nights before in Munich, performing what would be Nirvana's last gig.

From that day forward, I raised my barriers higher.

They finally closed in thirty-six days later.

Kurt's death was reported early in the morning on April 8. However, this time it was real. He was gone. There was no second phone call to correct the error. To turn a tragedy around. It was final. I hung up the phone and waited for the same shattering anguish to knock me to my knees again, but it never came. It was lodged deep within me, obstructed by the tragedy of a month prior, which had left me in a condition of divided emotional bewilderment. I don't remember anything about that day beyond turning on the television and hearing his name over and over. Kurt Cobain. Each time his name was mentioned, it gradually chipped away at the armor I had built to protect my heart. Kurt Cobain. I waited for the armor to be pierced, throwing me to the floor once more, but I refused to give in. I fought back, too frightened to experience that hurt again. Kurt was more than just a name to me; he was a friend, a parent, a son, an artist, and a human being, and he gradually became the center of our universe, the point around which our entire world revolved, yet he was still just a young guy with a lot to look forward to. We had a lot to look forward to.

That night, we all gathered at his house to attempt to console each other, but it was difficult to find solace because, no matter how many brushes with death he had, no one expected it to be this way. At least not me. There was shock, followed by despair, then remembering, and finally shock. I looked around the packed living room, seeing all the numerous lives he'd touched, each in their own unique way. Family members, old friends, and recent acquaintances are all mourning in their own ways. Life would never be the same for any of us, and this horrific incident had united us all permanently, leaving a wound that would undoubtedly scar. For years, I couldn't drive within a mile of that house on Lake Washington without experiencing debilitating dread from the sound of those cries.

The next day, I awoke, went to my kitchen, started making coffee, and it hit me. He isn't coming back. He's gone. But... I'm still here. I get to get up and live another day, whether it's good or horrible. That made no sense. How could someone just... disappear? It appeared unbelievable. And it's unfair.

Life quickly became a long list of firsts. This is my first cup of coffee since he disappeared. My first dinner after he vanished. My first telephone call. My first time driving, and so forth. Every step I took felt to be a step away from a time when he was alive, a series of experiences in which I had to relearn everything. I NEEDED TO LEARN TO LIVE AGAIN.

"Empathy!" Kurt said in his suicide letter, and there were times when I wished my heart could sense the sorrow he must have experienced. Ask for it to break. I'd try to wipe the tears from my eyes, cursing those filthy walls I'd built so high because they blocked me from feeling the emotions I urgently needed to feel. I cursed the voice on the phone who had informed me that Dad had gone prematurely, leaving me in this position of emotional bewilderment with no way of accessing the reservoir of sadness I needed to release. I was weighed down by the weight of it, knowing that grief was eating me alive, even if it was buried deeper than I could dig. I was anesthetized when all I wanted was to feel the surgery that would cure me.

I was ashamed at times because I couldn't feel, but I eventually realized that there is no right or wrong way to grieve. There is no textbook or handbook to turn to when in need of emotional support. It is an uncontrollable process, and you are utterly at its mercy, so you must surrender to it when it appears, regardless of your fear. Over time, I've come to terms with this. To this day, I am regularly hit with the same tremendous despair that sent me to the floor when I learned Kurt had passed away.

Is it time that determines the intensity of your sadness when you lose someone? Is emotional relevance solely influenced by the number of days you spend together? Kurt and I spent three and a half years together, a relatively short period of time in my life that defined and continues to define who I am now. I'll always be "that guy from Nirvana," and I'm proud of it.

But without my childhood best friend Jimmy Swanson, I would never have made it to Seattle, and his death has left a void in my life that is unlike any other.

On the morning of July 18, 2008, I learnt of Jimmy's death over the bedside phone in my Oklahoma City hotel room. He died in his sleep in the same North Springfield house where we first discovered the world of music as children, on the same couch where we would spend hours watching MTV, dreaming of one day living the lives of the renowned musicians we admired.

I hung up the phone, opened the blinds in my room, gazed at the sky, and communicated with him. We used to share notes in the high school halls between courses, but now we had to connect through spirit and prayer.

With Jimmy, I lost a piece of me. He was more than a person to me; he was my home, and while I could never let go of him, I did have to let go of who I was with him when he died. So came another round of firsts, but this time they proved more challenging because Jimmy and I had shared so many of life's firsts together. Like two conjoined twins separating. After years of sharing a body, I felt alone and questioned who I was now that I was on my own. I looked up to him, followed him, and coveted his ability to live his life so authentically. Everyone adored Jimmy because he was unlike anyone else on the planet. We both discovered individualism together, but we embraced it in different ways. As much as we both enjoyed music—and Jimmy tried his hand at playing, too—he was never inspired to follow through like me, preferring to remain in the background, cheering from the sidelines.

Jimmy's absence affected me deeply. Kurt died when I was only twenty-five years old, and I was unprepared for the struggles that were ahead. But Jimmy died when I was thirty-nine, and by that time, I had a much larger awareness of life, which helped me appreciate death more clearly. By that point, I had become a husband, a father, and the leader of a new band, with all of the duties that come with those positions. I was no longer a scrawny little child hiding behind a mane of hair and a massive drum equipment. As my emotions matured, they grew more focused and intense. I couldn't keep pushing things down and denying myself emotions. I knew there would be no miracle phone calls. I knew death was final. I knew that sorrow was a lengthy, unexpected journey. In a way, losing Kurt prepared me for losing Jimmy fourteen years later. Despite being completely different relationships, they were virtually equally influential, and both shaped the person I am now.

Kurt and Jimmy were not "family," but I welcomed them to be, and that invitation can sometimes be more intimate than a blood relationship. There was no biological responsibility here; we were bound by our similar spirits, love of music, and mutual admiration. You cannot pick your family, and when you lose them, there is a biological urge that requires a certain level of sorrow. However, with friends, you create your own bond, which in turn shapes your sadness, which can be felt even more deeply when they are gone. THOSE COULD BE ROOTS THAT ARE VERY DIFFICULT TO PULL.

These deaths continue to reverberate through my life, and I will never forget Kurt and Jimmy. There are simple reminders. A tune on the radio that Jimmy used to air-drum to while driving his old, beat-up Renault. Kurt would occasionally treat himself to pink strawberry milk from the petrol station. The smell of Jimmy's cheap Brut cologne, which he would apply to himself every morning for no one else to appreciate. Kurt frequently wore an Elmer Fudd hat to conceal his face from the public, as well as white-framed Jackie O spectacles, which became his hallmark. There seems to be a reminder everywhere I look, and I've gotten to the point where they no longer crush my heart; instead, they make me grin.

But when I sit down to play the drums, I feel Kurt the most. It's not often that I play the songs we did together, but when I sit on that stool, I can still see him in front of me, wrestling with his guitar while screaming his lungs raw into the microphone. When I gaze past my drums to the audience in front of me, his picture will be etched into my retinas in the same way that staring at the sun will.

He will always be present.

And every time I return to Virginia, I can feel Jimmy. He is in the trees we climbed as kids, in the cracks of the pathways we walked to primary school every morning, and in every gate we jumped to go around the neighborhood faster. There are times when I speak and the words are his, even though they are in my voice. And when I see him in my nightmares, he hasn't altered much. He's still my best friend.

Even though they are no longer with us, I carry these folks with me wherever I go.

And the walls are finally down.

THE HEARTBREAKER

"Dave, there's a phone call for you."

The studio engineer handed me the phone at the end of the long, curly line, and to my astonishment, it was Ron Stone calling, an acquaintance of my management whom we affectionately referred to as "Old School" due to his work with iconic musicians such as Bonnie Raitt and Neil Young. We'd never worked together before, so it was rare for him to call me directly, but even more unexpected was the news he had to share.

"Tom Petty is asking whether you will play drums for him on Saturday Night Live. .."

Bewildered, I responded, "Wait, what? Why me? The man could have any drummer in the world, and he's calling me." I mean, this is Tom Petty we're talking about, America's favorite Floridian, the embodiment of grassroots, working-class cool, the voice behind decades of classic rock hits, like "Breakdown," "American Girl," "Refugee," and "Free Fallin'."

His music was the soundtrack to a thousand hickeys, songs dripping with feel and groove, and he was calling the guy who only knew how to play the drums one of two ways: on or off. It made no sense.

Kurt's passing left me feeling lost. We all were. With our world ripped out from under us in such a devastating way, it was difficult to find any direction or lighthouse to help us navigate through the fog of enormous pain and loss. And the idea that Kurt, Krist, and I were all linked through music made any music feel bittersweet. What had once been my greatest joy had now become my greatest anguish, and I not only put away my instruments, but also turned off the radio, for fear that even the slightest music would elicit paralyzing grief. It was the first time I had ever rejected music. I simply couldn't afford to let it destroy my heart again.

In the months following his death, I felt like a fish stuck in a little bowl, feverishly swimming back and forth all day but never really getting anywhere. I was just twenty-five years old and had an entire life ahead of me, but in many ways, I felt like it had already ended. The thought of putting my drum equipment onstage behind simply another face was not only unpleasant, but also depressing. I was too young to fade away and too elderly to begin again. Sure, I could go out and join another band, but I'd always be known as "that guy from Nirvana," and I knew deep down that nothing could ever equal what Nirvana had given the world. That sort of stuff only occurs once in a lifetime.

After months of spinning my wheels in suffocating bouts of introspection, I decided I needed to get away from Seattle and clear my mind, so I traveled to a corner of the earth that I have always adored, a place of serenity and natural beauty where I hoped to find some healing from my broken life back home: the Ring of Kerry. The Ring of Kerry, a beautiful, secluded location in southwestern Ireland, is a return to the earth as it must have been thousands of years ago, before man carved it into concrete lots and busy thoroughfares. With miles of lush green fields overlooking coastal scenery and seaside settlements, there is a sense of serenity and tranquility that I sorely needed to review my life and begin again. I'd been there previously, driving from Dublin to Dingle with my mother and sister before Nirvana's 1992 Reading Festival play (our final performance in the UK), and I felt a connection to the countryside like no other place in the world. Maybe it was my mother's Irish roots, or maybe it was the pace of life, which reminded me of the rural sections of Virginia where I used to go hunting as a youngster, but whatever it was, I felt at ease in the calm and remoteness. I craved it right now.

One day, as I was driving my rental car through the potholes and deep ruts of a remote country road, I observed a teenage hitchhiker in the background. With his long, greasy hair and huge coat, I could tell this kid was a rocker who, despite being miles from the next town, really needed a ride to his destination. As I got closer, I intended to pick him up and give him a ride, but then I noticed something that made me reconsider.

He wore a Kurt Cobain T-shirt.

A flood of apprehension hit me like a jolt from an electric chair, and I sped past with my head down, hoping he wouldn't recognize me. My hands were shaking, and I felt as if I was about to vomit, dizzy from a debilitating panic attack. Here I was, desperately attempting to disappear in the most distant spot I could find to sort out a life that had been turned upside down only months before, and there was Kurt's face gazing back at me, almost as a warning that no matter how far I ran, I would never be able to forget the past.

This was the moment that altered everything.

I traveled back to the States and decided it was time to get back to work. Without a band or a solid strategy, I returned to where I felt most at ease: recording songs on my own. I learnt to do this by accident when I was twelve years old, with the help of two tape recorders, an old guitar, and some pots and pans. My method was straightforward: record a guitar part on one cassette, eject it, insert it into cassette player number two, press Play, record myself playing "drums" alongside the guitar part on another cassette, and so on. I was practically multitracking without even knowing it. I'd create crazy songs about my dog, school, and Ronald Reagan, but I was thrilled by the process, so I did it frequently. What is the best part? No one ever knew since I was terrified of letting anyone hear my prepubescent scream.

By the time I started hanging out and recording with my friend

Barrett Jones on the eight-track machine in his Virginia basement studio, I was used to laying down all of the instruments myself, systematically layering guitars, drums, and vocals as I had done as a child, though the RadioShack cassette players had been replaced by Barrett's professional reel-to-reel equipment. I never wanted to intrude (and never had enough money to pay him for engineering), so I'd wait until the conclusion of someone else's session and politely inquire, "Is there any extra tape at the end of the reel?" I'd like to try something. .." Knowing that this was a large task (and that I had already smoked most of his cannabis), I would rush from one instrument to the next, doing only one take on drums, one take on guitar, and one take on bass to avoid wasting Barrett's time or generosity. Then I'd go home and listen to my small experiment repeatedly, envisioning what I could achieve if I had more than fifteen minutes to record a song.

When Barrett relocated to Seattle and we found a house together, his studio was in MY basement, so I took advantage of its proximity and began writing songs that, while rudimentary and not yet ready for the public to hear, were a little more evolved. "Alone and Easy Target," "Floaty," "Weenie Beenie," "Exhausted," and "I'll Stick Around" were just a few of the dozens of songs that we recorded in our small basement on rainy days, and I was gradually building what would eventually become the Foo Fighters' catalog. Nirvana was in full stride at the time, and heaven knows we didn't need any songwriting assistance, so I kept the songs to myself, remembering that old drummer joke, "What was the last thing the drummer said before getting kicked out of the band?" 'Hey, fellas, I wrote a song that I believe we should play!!'"

With nothing to lose and nowhere to run, I returned from Ireland and decided to schedule six days at Robert Lang Studios, a cutting-edge facility built into the side of a massive hill overlooking the Puget Sound. I had previously recorded there, including Nirvana's last session, where we recorded our final song, "You Know You're Right," earlier that year. Robert Lang, the studio's eccentric, oddball owner, decided to build a recording facility beneath his house in the early 1970s and spent fifteen years digging deeper and deeper into the hill, hauling thousands of dump trucks' worth of dirt away and creating what can only be described as a massive concrete bunker with a great collection of vintage microphones. The most notable variation from other studios was the use of marble and stone in the tracking rooms. Rather than the warm absorption of natural wood and acoustically corrected baffles, his rooms featured the merciless reflection of hard stone, which gave the music a far more "live" quality. Nirvana chose to record there because, during our initial tour of the studio, Bob showed us a little slab that he believed had a vision of a saintlike figure, a halo, a dove, and the resurrection descending. That was enough for Krist Novoselic and me to say, "Oh, we're definitely going to record here. ..This man is WILD." Plus, it was so close to my house that I could drive there in my lawnmower-powered go-kart.

I scheduled October 17 to 22, 1994, and began to prepare. I chose the fifteen songs that I thought were the best of the innumerable recordings Barrett and I had made over the years, gathered the equipment, and devised a plan: four songs per day for four days, with the final two days for vocals and mixing. I could pull it off if I recorded at my usual tempo, rushing from instrument to instrument, doing only one or two takes before moving on to the next. I devised a calendar, determining which songs to record on which days, and rehearsed tirelessly, knowing there was little time to spare. Six days in the studio felt like an eternity to me, but I needed to prove that I could fulfill the goal I had set for myself, which was the entire point of this new project.

Barrett and I put in the gear on Monday morning, made coffee, collected sounds, and were ready to record by midday. First up was a new song called "This Is a Call," which I rushed through in one take, then switched to the guitar and finished swiftly before moving on to the bass for one run. Within 45 minutes, the instrumental was complete. The next song was "I'll Stick Around." It was the same drill: drums, guitar, bass, and it was completed in 45 minutes. Then "Big Me," followed by "Alone and Easy Target". ..By the conclusion of the first day, we'd completed our four-song quota with plenty of time left over, and my lofty ambition no longer seemed so daunting. I really felt. ..good.

This was more than simply a recording session for me; it was genuinely therapeutic. A continuation of life. This was what I needed to defibrillate my heart and restore its natural rhythm: an electric pulse to rekindle my love and faith in music. Beyond simply picking up an instrument and feeling industrious or prolific, I could see through the windshield rather than in the rearview mirror.

By the end of the week, I had not only completed the fifteen songs (actually recording them in the order of the eventual album), but I had also agreed to perform with Tom Petty on Saturday Night Live, a step back into my former life that I was no longer afraid to take. There was light at the end of the tunnel now. Neither of these activities was considered a permanent life direction; they were simply tiny steps forward. There was no vision for what would happen next. Not quite yet.

I took the master tape of Barrett's rough mixes to a tape duplication shop in downtown Seattle, where I decided to make a hundred cassette copies of my new project, intending to give them to friends, family, and anyone who was curious about what "that guy from Nirvana" had been up to since the band disbanded. I had kept my songs a secret for much of my life, but now I was ready to share them with the world because I was more proud of them than anything I had ever recorded. Barrett's amazing production skills provided emotional fulfillment in addition to sound benefits. I had eventually surfaced with an exaggerated gasp, as if I had been held underwater for too long.

Even though I had played every instrument on that cassette (with the exception of one guitar track played by my friend Greg Dulli of the Afghan Whigs, whom I handed a guitar to while he was visiting the studio one day), I was mortified at the prospect of calling it a "solo" endeavor. I couldn't envision "the Dave Grohl Experience" being a moniker that would send people flocking to the record stores, and to be honest, I knew that the link to Nirvana would much overwhelm any listener's objectivity. So I decided to take a more incognito approach, drawing influence from Stewart Copeland, the Police drummer, and his 1980 "solo" project Klark Kent. The Police were an emerging band at the time, so Stewart decided to record under the moniker Klark Kent, playing all of the instruments solo, as I had done. I enjoyed the mystery of it. Having been a UFO enthusiast my entire life, I selected a simple phrase from a book I was reading at the time, Above Top Secret, which was a collection of UFO sighting reports and military testimonies dating back to the early 1940s. In a chapter discussing unidentified craft over Europe and the Pacific during World War II, I came across a term used by the military as a nickname for these unexplained blazing balls of light, which I found intriguing enough. It sounded not only like a bunch of people, but almost like a gang: the Foo Fighters.

And then there was Tom. He was just how I had imagined him to be, completely laid-back and effortlessly cool, and when he said hello, the voice of a thousand high school dances poured out of his mouth like thick molasses. Within a few minutes, any nerves I had from this rock and roll fantasy camp reverie had subsided, and we began to play. I couldn't suppress my excitement, so I believe I was using more muscle than usual, since the band was nearly cringing from the cannon-level volume of my drums. We spent the afternoon jamming, hanging out, and casually getting to know each other in between takes, and by the end of the day, they treated me like an honorary Heartbreaker. I felt as if we were a band. And that was a feeling I hadn't had in a long time.

The show was excellent. We rocked both songs with rhythm and passion, and after only a week and a half of knowing each other, I was starting to feel unexpectedly at ease in the band's laid-back dynamic, which I had never felt in the three and a half years I was in Nirvana. The awkward dysfunction of Nirvana certainly made a lot of noise, but the sense of family and community in the Heartbreakers' camp appeared far healthier and less chaotic. This was just what I needed to calm my past traumas, and it served as a terrific reminder that music represents joy, life, and celebration. This was the ideal one-off to get me back on my feet, I reasoned.

Tom then asked if I'd consider doing it again.

I adored Tom's music and would have had a great time playing it night after night, unfortunately... They were not mine. We spoke over the phone once again, and Tom indicated that they traveled extremely well. I'd have my own bus, and the schedules were much more relaxed than the arduous van runs I was used to. Everything sounded so wonderful. Nearly too perfect. I was 25 years old and still hungry, not ready to settle for a "sure thing." I still had the restless energy of a youngster, eager to thrive in the unknown, even if it was frightening at times.

So I politely rejected, deciding that the cardboard box in the back of my vehicle held the key to a new existence. It wasn't a sure thing, but nothing is.

RIP Tom Petty, 1950-2017.

THIS IS WHAT I WANTED

"Mom . . . we're having a girl."

My mother's voice cracked as she started crying. "Oh, David...," she whispered. "Oh my goodness . . ." There was a long gap as she put down the phone to wipe the tears of pride from her cheeks, and as I stood in my backyard, trying to understand what had just come out of my mouth, it struck me. I was about to have a daughter. My mom was pleased. I was shocked.

I had always known that someday I would be a father, but it would be a long time after my touring and traveling days were done. As my father had stated years before, "You know this isn't going to last, right?" I had anticipated that the music would simply stop and I would resume a life of domestic anonymity. I'd seen others attempt to raise a family on the road (preach, Steve Perry!) However, due to my traditional upbringing, I felt that thought to be excessively rickety and unstable. The sight of a Pack 'n Play next to a table full of alcohol and Jägermeister always made me uneasy.

It wasn't until the Foo Fighters were asked to perform at Neil Young's Bridge School Benefit in 2000 that I understood these two worlds might coexist. The Bridge School Benefit was an annual weekend-long concert organized by Neil and Pegi Young to raise funds for the Bridge School, a nonprofit organization that Pegi founded to provide a place for their son Ben, who has cerebral palsy, and other children with severe speech and physical impairments to receive language and communication assistance. Each year, the concert was hosted at the Shoreline Amphitheatre just outside of San Francisco, with fantastic lineups such as Springsteen, Dylan, McCartney, Petty, the Beach Boys, Pearl Jam, and Metallica (to name a few), all doing acoustic sets while the students sat behind them onstage. These shows raised millions of dollars, and the sense of love and joy at those events was unlike anything I had ever experienced. Every single person in attendance was there to support the children, and I was persuaded that the community energy of so much positivity in one area had its own healing power.

The weekend traditionally started with a BBQ at Neil's residence on Broken Arrow Ranch, a vast, rustic 140-acre paradise in Redwood City that he bought in 1970. Neil would invite all of the musicians to supper the night before the show. While we drove down the winding mountain roads deep in the redwoods toward his home, I imagined a lavish catered gathering, tables lined with rock and roll royalty rattling their gleaming cutlery, laps adorned with linen napkins, while they exchanged mythical folklore from the past. That could not have been farther from the truth. When we arrived at the gate, there was a hand-painted sign that screamed DON'T SPOOK THE HORSE hanging from the decaying fence, and once inside the property, we had another ten-minute drive over twisting hills before we saw the modest house, lit up like a Christmas tree in the distance. It appeared to be the product of a crazed survivalist with a fondness for tree houses, replete with bellows and a tall teepee in the yard. There is no valet parking or reception; you simply stroll right in.

As I entered the kitchen, I was greeted with a loving hug from Pegi, who was cutting vegetables beside the sink. She handed me a coat from the mudroom in case it became cold outside, but told me to "check the pockets for mice." David Crosby was seated near the fireplace. Brian Wilson was roaming around aimlessly, looking for his wife. Tom Petty's band was playing on the porch, and Neil's kids were hanging out with everyone. This was not a formal rock and roll event. This was a home. This was a family.

THIS IS WHAT I WANT, AND I CAN NOW SEE HOW IT IS POSSIBLE.

As my mother regained her composure after learning she would have a granddaughter, I told her that, while I had always known I would become a father eventually, I had never envisioned having a female. By no means am I a cigar-chomping, NASCAR-watching, Sunday-afternoon-armchair-quarterback type of person, but what could I possibly offer a daughter? How do you tune a kick drum and catalog your Slayer bootlegs? I was at a loss. And then, as she always did, my mother delivered some of her well-earned knowledge, which has since proven to be one of my life's most incontrovertible truths: "The relationship between a father and daughter can be one of the most special relationships in any girl's life." She knew this because of her relationship with her father, a military man of charm and with whom everyone adored before his unexpected death when she was in her thirties. I never had the pleasure of meeting him, but from what I've heard, he was a kind man who had a unique connection with my mother. Though I was still afraid, I felt slightly relieved. Maybe cataloging Slayer bootlegs together would be fun.

As the months passed, Jordyn and I began to prepare for the new baby, preparing her room, purchasing for all of the required supplies, and eventually deciding on the name Violet (after my mother's mother, Violet Hanlon). I was given a library of books to study on topics ranging from sleep training (which is a farce because they eventually sleep-train you, making it impossible to sleep past six a.m. for the rest of your life) to swaddling (I'm bad enough at rolling joints; how could I successfully roll a child?) to diaper changing (which I may hold a land speed record in by this point). I was taking a crash course in fatherhood, or at least the logistical side of things.

Violet was born after a long and tough labor to the music of the Beatles in the background, screaming with a predefined vocal capability that made the Foo Fighters sound like the Carpenters. After she was cleaned up and placed under the small Arby's heat-lamp bed, I pressed my face against hers, looked into her massive blue eyes, and said, "Hey, Violet, it's Dad." She suddenly stopped screaming and locked eyes with me. She recognized my voice. We stared at each other in silence for our initial introduction, and I smiled and spoke to her as if I'd known her all my life. I'm pleased to announce that when we lock eyes, it still feels the same.

This was a love I'd never felt before. Being a famous artist brings with it an unavoidable sense of uneasiness that causes you to question love. Do they adore me? Or do they adore "it"? You are showered with superficial love and affection on a regular basis, giving you a feeling similar to a sugar high, but your heart falls as the rush fades. Is it possible for someone to observe a musician and not associate them with their instrument? Is that an aspect of the identity that the other person values? Regardless, it is a risky and slippery slope to question love, but one thing is certain: there is nothing purer than unconditional love between a parent and their kid.

My mother was correct: being a parent to a daughter was the most special relationship of my life. I quickly learned how to do a smudge-free manicure, knot the perfect ponytail, and identify every Disney princess based solely on the color of her clothing. This was simple, I thought.

THEN CAME THE HARD PART: BALANCING THE NEW AND THE OLD.

I recall the first time I had to leave Violet behind on tour. As she slept, I stood above her cot and started crying. How could I possibly leave this small marvel behind? I had to drag myself away, beginning a lifelong habit of leaving half of my heart at home. At this point, all of the band members were reproducing like rabbits, and our tour schedules were now governed by people who couldn't even swallow solid food, so six-week tours were reduced to two weeks at most. As much as touring with a rock band is the best fucking job on earth, it can be exhausting, but the moment you get home after a few weeks away, you are handed a crying kid and are officially on daddy duty 24/7. This, of course, is partly to relieve your wife of the mother chores that she was burdened with from sunrise to sunset while you were out shotgunning beers with your best buddies (cue little anger), but it is also because you feel compelled to overcompensate for your absence. You are constantly haunted by the idea that your child will suffer long-term psychological consequences as a result of your absence, so when you get home, you are HOME. After a few years, you begin to discover the balance and realize that the two worlds CAN coexist. So why not try it again?

This time, I expected a boy.

"Mom . . . we're having another girl."

To clarify, I never had a gender preference, although I did want to name a child Harper Bonebrake Grohl. So we named her Harper (never got the Bonebrake past the goalie), and she was born just two days after Violet's third birthday. The sense of tremendous paternal love was revived, and now I had two children to adore: Violet, who walks and talks at a level way beyond her age, and Harper (my spitting image), who coos in my lap and never stops smiling. This was a home. This was a family. This is just what I wanted.

As I witnessed each stage of their development, it was difficult not to imagine my parents doing the same. I have limited recollections of these years in my life, the majority of which were spent with my mother, who lavished me with unconditional affection, rather than with my father. My parents split when I was six years old, leaving me to be raised by my mother, and now that I am a father, I struggle to understand this separation. How could he not want to spend every waking moment bouncing me on his lap, pushing me in the swing, or reading me books before bedtime? Was it that he did not want to? Or perhaps he didn't know how? Perhaps this was the root of my anxiety of being an absent parent, my tendency to overcompensate whenever I returned home after being away. As fortunate as I was to be raised by my beautiful mother, I could see how my damaged relationship with my father and his absence in my childhood had long-term psychological consequences, and I was determined not to create those for my own children.

We began to travel the world with our daughters, and I no longer felt strange about a backstage full of children (though they were in their own dressing room so they wouldn't be playing next to the beer and Jägermeister), because no matter where we were on the planet, if we were together, it felt like home. My father had warned me that my life would never last, but what I saw that night at Neil Young's house was music and family entwined. It was conceivable, after all.

Ophelia was born just down the hall from where I once ran for my life from that Slovakian Hulk Hogan dressed in Crocs and baby-blue scrubs, and a few days later, we invited Paul McCartney and his wife Nancy around to meet the baby. This was a historic event for a variety of reasons, but one item struck me as particularly memorable. Violet and Harper were definitely aware that Paul was a member of the Beatles, but they had no concept what that meant in the grand scheme of musical history. To them, Paul was simply our musician buddy Paul, and I witnessed that when those false notions are removed, there is a purity of spirit and unconditional love. I, of course, spent the hour before his arrival hiding the mounds of Beatles material I had in the house (you never know how much Beatles memorabilia you have until a Beatle comes to visit), but the kids had no overblown expectations of who he was.

As they were leaving and we were saying our goodbyes, Paul saw the piano down the hall and couldn't resist. He sat down and began playing "Lady Madonna" as I stood stunned, hearing a voice adored by the world echo throughout my own home, which was suddenly filled with my own family. Harper vanished for a moment before returning with a coffee cup full with spare change and placing it on the piano as a tip jar for Sir Paul. We fell about the room laughing, and he encouraged her to sit on the bench next to him for her first piano lesson. He showed her the keys and which notes they were, and they started playing together while Paul sang, "We're playing a song... we're playing a song..."

The next morning, as I was preparing breakfast in the kitchen, I heard the piano again, the same music that Paul and Harper had performed the night before. I looked around the corner and saw Harper alone on the stool, her tiny hands playing the same chords in perfect rhythm, and I understood exactly how she felt: inspired by Paul. Because I previously felt the same way. The difference was that his voice came from the tiny turntable on my bedroom floor, rather than there alongside me on the piano bench as I played along with him.

The circle was complete.

This was a home. This was a family. This is just what I wanted.

A few days later, my father died. We had lost touch over the last year of his life, but when I learned of his sickness the month before Ophelia's birth, I rushed to see him, knowing it would be the last time we ever met. We sat and chatted in the same Warren, Ohio, hospital where I was born, exchanging life updates as I congratulated him on his long white hair and beard, which had nearly overtaken mine. When I told him I was about to become a father again, he congratulated me and wished me the best of luck. When it was time to leave, I kissed his hand and murmured, "Okay, Dad. I will see you later. "I love you."

He grinned and added, "I love you, too, David."

PART 4

CRUISING

CROSSING THE BRIDGE TO WASHINGTON

"I'll see you down there, dude!"

Paralyzed, with my back against the wall of a long hallway below in the White House, I couldn't believe what I was hearing.

George W. Bush, the president of the United States of America, had just addressed me as "dude."

Frozen in shock, I politely waved as Secret Service agents whisked him away, then continued on my mission to find the coatroom to get my very pregnant wife's winter jacket so that we could head down to the Kennedy Center Honors, where I would be performing the classic "Who Are You" for a star-studded tribute to the Who, which President Bush would be watching from his center seat in the balcony.

How on Earth did I get here?

Since 1978, the Kennedy Center Honors have been regarded as America's most prominent performing arts awards program, honoring individuals in music, dance, theater, opera, film pictures, and television for their lifetime contributions to American culture. Being involved in any manner is an honor in and of itself. The event, a virtual who's who of Washington, DC's most recognizable faces, is actually a weekend of multiple gatherings, ranging from dinner at the State Department the night before to an awards presentation in the White House's East Room the afternoon of the show, but the festivities always began with the Chairman's Luncheon at a hotel. It's a reasonably informal occasion, similar to a brunch buffet at your cousin's wedding, except instead of sharing the salad tongs with your eccentric uncle, you pass them like a baton to former Secretary of State Madeleine Albright. The ridiculousness of this most strange situation was difficult to ignore, and I found myself attempting to maintain a straight face while surrounded by the people who made the world's most important decisions, fumbling with smoked salmon slipping off their bagels. Most of the award ceremonies I attend make me feel as if I'm crashing the party, with security escorting me out to the parking lot after only one drink. But I've never been afraid to strike up discussions with the most unexpected folks, no matter how out of my element I am.

For security reasons, all performers are required to be shuttled to and from the Kennedy Center on one of those large buses that tourists usually fill to visit Washington's most popular attractions, but instead of gangs of blue-haired seniors from the Midwest, the bus is filled with America's most recognizable artists, usually breaking into a roaring version of "99 Bottles of Beer on the Wall" (take it from me, the song really acquires a whole new life when sung by St It's seldom a long trip to the gig, but just enough time to get to know these old faces and become good friends, swapping anecdotes about storied careers and getting hearing aid advice from the finest (thank you, Herbie).

Rehearsals for the shows take place in one of the several chambers off to the side of the main stage, which have definitely witnessed their fair share of history over the years. Growing up just across the bridge in Virginia, I was familiar with the Kennedy Center, having watched many shows and done numerous school field excursions to view the stunning display of modern architecture overlooking the Potomac River, but the backstage area was new to me. As I strolled through the corridors behind the stage, I attempted to visualize all of the voices that had filled these sacred chambers since their inception in 1971, asking myself once more, "How on earth did I get here?" This structure was intended for America's most prominent entertainers, not former DC punk rock gangsters.

As much as it's regarded as a nonpolitical event, a rare opportunity for people from both sides of the aisle to set aside their differences and share a drink in the name of culture and the arts, there is an unavoidable tension that pervades the proceedings, as if all of the attendees are small children who have been told to behave on the school playground. I certainly did not agree with all of the ideas and values that some of these individuals spent their days debating, so I followed my mother's advice and avoided the three things that we were always taught not to discuss at the dinner table: money, politics, and religion. This was a weekend when everyone recognized each other as more than just Democrats or Republicans. We were all humans first and foremost, and nothing brings people together like music and art.

For some odd reason, I was asked to salute the Who for their achievement at the ultra-formal State Department dinner the night before the event. This was not the type of blathering, inebriated tirade you'd give from a barstool in your local dive; rather, it was a dignified speech congratulating the winner of this highest distinction on all of their accomplishments. Even in front of a room full of orators. Not to be taken lightly. I was assigned a speechwriter, who generously met me backstage during rehearsal and conducted a brief interview with me to generate ideas for my speech. After a brief talk, she thanked me and promised to get my speech ready before dinner that night. I would have wanted to compose my own, but I didn't want to rock the boat, so I left it to the professionals.

Later, while I was getting back into my penguin suit at the hotel, my speech arrived, and to my dismay, it was written in a rudimentary sort of "dude-speak" to make it appear as if I had written it myself (I assume). Oh my gosh, I thought. I cannot read this! As the son of a former Capitol Hill speechwriter and distinguished journalist, I would eternally betray my father's reputation as a guy of knowledge, wit, and Washington charm. I also felt obligated to follow the program and offer these lines to the crowd in a selfless act of comic relief. Fuck, I thought. MADELEINE ALBRIGHT WILL THINK I'M A MORON.

Filing down the receiving line, I was already dreading my time at the platform as I shook hands with current Secretary of State Condoleezza Rice, which was yet another thing I never imagined would happen. Looking around the room full of scholars and intellectual titans, my old childhood concern about being labeled as stupid surfaced, and I began to doubt myself. All of the pomp and grandeur on display in the ballroom was undoubtedly fun to see, and I've never been one to turn down the chance to embarrass myself for a mortified chuckle, but this was being thrown to the goddamned lions. Please order a cocktail.

As I sat at my table with other senators and cabinet members, I held that awful speech in my hands like a string of prayer beads, counting down the minutes till my most heinous public death. I sat and watched as each speaker, one by one, delivered a lengthy, beautiful speech worthy of any inaugural or State of the Union address... knowing that I would soon be the only jackass in the room to use the term "dude."

As Bob Schieffer, one of America's most beloved television journalists and debate moderators, toasted the legendary country singer George Jones, I sat in front of my uneaten dinner, astounded by his ability to be outrageously funny, deeply emotional, perfectly informative, and brilliantly poetic all at once off-the-cuff, speaking with a relaxed and confident tone and commanding the room with no prepared speech to refer to. Okay. Fuck it. There was no way I was going to read the speech that had been prepared for me. Not following Bob Schieffer!

It was time to think of something quickly.

With barely a few minutes to spare, I came up with an idea: The Who's distinctive reversal of musical roles distinguished them from other bands. Keith Moon's lyrical drumming made him more like the vocalist, Pete Townshend's solid rhythm guitar made him more like the drummer, John Entwistle's unconventional bass soloing made him more like the lead guitarist, and Roger Daltrey's muscular vocals brought everything together like a conductor for a fire orchestra. This might work! I thought. In any case, I had nothing to lose because it was already far superior to the crumpled speech clasped in my sweaty fist. I had built my entire career around one basic rule: you fake it until you make it. My name was called, so I rose up, left the crumpled speech next to my cold, untouched coq au vin, and walked to the stage.

I must admit that I was no Bob Schieffer that night, but I was able to pull it off without receiving any rotten tomatoes or a single "dude." Madeleine Albright may even have smiled at me.

We all sat in the East Room the next afternoon for the White House celebration, when President Bush presented the recipients with their colorful medals. Of course, I had only visited the White House as a visitor before, so this was another watershed experience for me. But let me tell you something: given the hundreds of years of history that have created our globe from behind those walls, it's really not that big of a joint. We sat quietly in our little folding chairs, crammed together like commuters on the morning bus, while the president wrapped the rainbow-ribboned medals around the necks of that year's recipients: Morgan Freeman, George Jones, Barbra Streisand, Twyla Tharp, and the Who. I FELT LIKE I WAS SEEING HISTORY, WHICH MADE ME ASK MYSELF, HOW ON EARTH DID I GET HERE?

At this time, the only thing left to do before heading to the gig was take a photo with the president and First Lady in front of the White House Christmas tree. This was a decision that required more than a moment to consider. To put it gently, my personal politics did not fit with those of the present administration, therefore I was uneasy about taking a picture with the president. Even though this weekend was intended to be free of political polarization, an opportunity to come together and celebrate the arts, it was tough to put all of my politics aside, even if just for a photo in front of a bedazzled Christmas tree. My heart was once again filled with questions. What Am I doing here?

I thought of my father. What will he do? As a devout Republican, he had spent decades cultivating lifelong friendships with folks from both sides of the aisle and could enjoy a large martini with practically anyone. On weekends, dad would occasionally take me to Nathan's, a corner saloon in Georgetown where scores of seersucker barflies would gather to drink, laugh, and debate—but most importantly, to coexist. I'd sit at the bar, drinking my ginger ale, listening to the booming voices of these Beltway news addicts, agreeing to disagree on current events and saving any actual debate for when the House met Monday morning. This was the Washington, DC I was raised to know, a city where individuals with opposite viewpoints could engage in courteous discourse without escalating into a barroom brawl. A place that has now unfortunately perished.

Jordyn and I opted to wait in line for the picture. Surrounded by marines in dress uniforms, we were ultimately taken into a room where the president and First Lady stood like cardboard cutouts in front of a huge Christmas tree, and we greeted them with smiles and firm handshakes. First impressions? The president was taller than I expected, and the First Lady had stunning blue eyes. "Where are you from???" the president exclaimed in my face with the zeal of a military drill sergeant. Surprised, I responded, "Uhhh... uhhhh... just over that bridge right there!" as I pointed to the South Lawn. When I told him I was there to sing a Who song at the Kennedy Center, he grinned, the picture was taken, and we were whisked out the door faster than you can say "We won't get fooled again."

I can only believe he recognized me in the downstairs corridor later that evening because I was the only one in attendance with hair past my collar, but I had to giggle when he triumphantly called me the one thing I had gone to such lengths to avoid saying the night before. If Nathan's bar in Georgetown was still open, I think the two of us would have a very exciting Sunday afternoon.

LIFE WAS PICKING UP SPEED

LIFE WAS PICKING UP SPEED.

2009 was a fantastic year. It all started with my fortieth birthday party, which was held at the Medieval Times theme restaurant in Anaheim, California, a massive equestrian arena where you could watch fake knights with fake English accents joust while eating greasy turkey legs with your bare hands and drinking Coors Light from BeDazzled chalices. Forever immortalized in Jim Carrey's greatest film, The Cable Guy, it is the most absurd, hilarious, and downright embarrassing dining experience known to man, and apparently not somewhere a grown man would typically celebrate another trip around the sun, which I didn't realize until the fake king's voice came booming over the PA with a few announcements. "Ladies and gentlemen, tonight we celebrate a few birthdays! Eddie is turning seven. Tommy is turning ten! And Dave is turning... forty?

I sat behind my kit and made minor tweaks while John warmed up his fingers on the bass, ripping the most uncanny phrases with ease, and then I joined in with his rhythm, locking in so perfectly and effortlessly that I thought to myself, WOW! I'm fucking killing it!! But I soon discovered that it wasn't me making the drums sound good; it was John. His ability to lock into the drums and follow every beat was incredible, making the groove flow so much smoother and stronger than anything I'd ever experienced with another bassist. That was the moment I knew this experiment was going to work. When Josh joined in, it only took a few seconds for us to realize this was meant to be. There was no going back now.

We jammed for a few days, getting to know each other while ordering out from another medieval-themed restaurant across the street, Kids Castle (or, as we kindly referred to it, Kids Asshole), feeling each other out and writing a few riffs, eventually coming up with a master plan to pursue this new musical union: we would meet in L.A. for two weeks to write and record, disperse and retreat to our corners for a small break, and then reconvene and continue to build an arsen It was official.

LIFE WAS PICKING UP SPEED

Meanwhile, the day job beckoned. After a year and a half on the road, the Foo Fighters were asked to create and record a new song to include in the tracklist to help sell it (otherwise known as "the song on the greatest hits record that is neither great nor a hit"). Discussions about how, when, and with whom we would record began, and now that I was technically in two bands, this scheduling required some logistical work. I wasn't sure how or when we could do it, but I knew exactly who I wanted to do it with: my old friend Butch Vig.

Butch and I had a long and strong relationship, but we hadn't worked together since 1991, when Nirvana's Nevermind was recorded. For years, I was hesitant to collaborate with Butch again for fear that the lengthy shadow that Nirvana had put over me following Kurt's death would undermine the validity of my own music. Whatever we recorded together would only be compared to what we had done previously, which has been a cross I have had to bear since we met. As much as I adored Butch, and despite the fact that he is one of the best producers of all time and the drummer of alt-rock legends Garbage, I didn't want his weight to overshadow what should have been a lovely reunion. Butch's approach is straightforward: obtain huge sounds, play big riffs, and write a big tune. That is it. It was often difficult to determine if he was actually working because he is so laid-back and relaxed that you forgot you're on the clock. With his thick Wisconsin accent and kind studio manner, it was easy to forget that he had produced some of the most successful rock albums of all time for Nirvana, the Smashing Pumpkins, and Green Day, to name a few. But, after some significant soul searching, I decided to disregard what the naysayers would say and contribute As with most things in my life, I revel in the absurdity of it all and seize every bizarre moment, so what better place to gather 150 of my closest friends, all seated in the "Blue Knight" section of the arena, drunkenly cheering on our noble chevalier with bloodthirsty abandon and praying for a kill? And what better time to launch a band than the night I brought Led Zeppelin's bassist, John Paul Jones, to my old friend Josh Homme, to kick off our new, top-secret project, Them Crooked Vultures.

I met Josh in the early 1990s while he was playing guitar in one of my favorite bands of all time, Kyuss, and we had since toured the world together with his band Queens of the Stone Age, which I had even briefly joined, recording their album Songs for the Deaf and playing some of the most explosive shows of my life. Josh has "the thing," an indefinable, unspoken, magical ability that is truly one-of-a-kind, and whenever we played together, the result was always like the hypnotic wave of a murmuration of starlings, the music effortlessly flowing from one direction to the next with grace, never losing its tight rhythm. Our onstage improvisation resembled that of two old friends finishing each other's sentences while giggling wildly behind the audience's back at our musical inside jokes. In essence, it was a perfect match, and we would seize any opportunity to work together.

We discussed a side project from time to time, generally when we were exhausted by our day jobs' demands and obligations, or when our bands met on tour. We'd sit about with cartons of cigarettes and gallons of backstage cocktails, thinking about something crazy, loose, and wonderful. Josh was also a drummer, so we could quickly switch instruments and try to go as far away from the sound of Queens and the Foos as possible. But, beyond any musical prediction, we knew we'd have a great time, and after a year and a half on the road playing "Learn to Fly" every single night, the promise of something pleasant was much needed to keep me from quitting music entirely and being the lousy roofer I was destined to be.

Around the same time, I was asked to present a GQ Outstanding Achievement Award to the members of Led Zeppelin (let that painfully obvious sentiment sink in for a moment), so I called Josh and asked if I could mention our secret project to John Paul Jones, the greatest, grooviest bassist in rock and roll history. "You know John Paul Jones?" he inquired. It turns out I did, as I recorded with him once on the Foo Fighters' album In Your Honor in 2004. He also led the orchestra during a Food Grammy performance. I thought him to be not only friendly and down-to-earth, but also a brilliant musician. Furthermore, he had worked as a producer for fringe musicians such as the amazing Butthole Surfers and Diamanda Galás. The guy was not afraid to become crazy, to say the least, so there was optimism that he would agree to our bizarre plan. If Josh and I could combine our powers with the all-powerful John Paul Jones, we would undoubtedly form a "supergroup" (a stupid word that we rejected). Josh and I concluded, what the hell, it was worth a shot, and before long, I was standing face to face with John at the award ceremony, timidly whispering the suggestion into his ear. He didn't say yes, but he didn't say no either, so we agreed to stay in touch via email and see if we could work something out. I flew home excited about the prospect of really playing drums with a man who had previously played with the drummer who had inspired me the most. I could only hope that he would accept our proposal, but I wasn't holding my breath because, well, he was John Paul Jones.

Lo and behold, John decided to travel to Los Angeles to see if we had the chemistry that I had hoped for, and his arrival coincided with my fantastically juvenile birthday party, so I invited him along for a medieval feast of greasy fast food delights. Poor man, he was about to be thrown into a nauseating, Americanized version of the Middle Ages while his host and future bandmate became cross-eyed drunk, smoking joints in the men's room like a high school delinquent between staged jousting bouts. If he can get through this night of lowbrow theater and juvenile shenanigans without rushing back to LAX, we might have a shot at something amazing. Bless his heart, he patiently endured my immaturity, and we met a few days later at Josh's studio, Pink Duck, for our first jam session.

The calendars came out, and no matter how hard we tried to locate free time, the Foos sessions had to compete with previously booked Them Crooked Vultures sessions. We figured if I recorded with the Foos from 11 a.m. to 6 p.m. and then raced to the Vultures' studio from 7 p.m. to midnight, I'd be able to do it. No problem, I thought. I will sleep when I die! After all, a couple additional cups of coffee per day couldn't hurt! So, in order to achieve this insane goal, I quickly increased my consumption of that dirty, black daily grind to dangerously high levels.

Oh, and I had another child.

Harper Willow Grohl was born April 17, 2009. She was a screaming bundle of joy from day one, so wonderful and adorable. My understanding of love grew tenfold with her arrival, and I was once again a proud parent. I've always had a deep appreciation for life, but my new daughter made me love it even more, waking up every morning delighted to see her gorgeous face, no matter how sleep deprived I was. As any parent will confirm, the miracle of a newborn takes precedence over everything else in your life, and you forget about your own existence because you are fully focused on theirs, an ethos that my mother undoubtedly showed during my upbringing. I was happy to now have two lovely girls and would jump at any chance to be with them, day or night, no matter how weary I was from my insane schedule of rushing from one studio to the next all day, drinking coffee like it was an Olympic competition.

LIFE WAS PICKING UP SPEED.

I returned to Los Angeles and immediately contacted my doctor. "Dude, I've been having chest pains," I informed him. "Are you having them right now??" he inquired, appearing more concerned than usual. "Ummm... kinda...," I responded. He urged me to get in the car and hurry to his office right away, so I accelerated out the door and parted traffic like Moses. I burst into his office and was soon lying on a table, examined and prodded, and connected up like a vintage synthesizer. He looked at the paper printout from the EKG as it spilled onto the floor and stated, "Hmmmm... not seeing anything here... let's get you on the treadmill and then we'll do an ultrasound." I was transferred to another floor, coated in small electro-patches, and instructed to jog on a treadmill like the Six Million Dollar Man. Then I jumped onto a table and was slathered in gel while they used an ultrasound wand to watch my heart pulse. "Hmmmm . . . not seeing anything here . . . let's get you over to Cedars for a CT scan . . ." I was beginning to feel like the little girl in The Exorcist, forced to test after test when it was all a simple demonic possession. Perhaps I needed a priest.

After consulting with the doctor at Cedars and finding no symptoms of genuine concern, he advised me to take it easy. As much as I felt invincible, I was not a superhero, and I needed to take care of myself in order to care for those I loved. My enthusiasm for life may be overwhelming at times, to the point where I pushed myself too far, but if I wanted to stay around for a while, I needed to be more aware of my mortal boundaries. What is his prescription? "Play drums only three times a week, have a glass of wine before bed, and lay off the coffee."

Two out of three isn't bad. DECAF BLOWS.

AND LIFE WAS STILL PICKING UP SPEED.

INSPIRED, YET AGAIN

"Excuse me, are you Dave Grohl?"

Standing at the sidewalk outside the LAX departure terminal, waiting to board my aircraft to Seattle, I took a deep drag on my cigarette and nodded. "Yep." The young man grinned and continued, "I read in an interview that you had always wanted to meet Little Richard. Is this true?"

"Certainly," I responded. "He's the originator."

"Well, he's my dad," he explained.

I leaped back, threw my cigarette to the ground, and shook the man's hand firmly, honored and amazed to have met the son of rock and roll's greatest pioneer.

Would you like to meet him? "He's right here in the car..."

I could scarcely talk. This was the moment I'd been waiting for. There has never been anyone more significant to me on God's green earth than Little Richard. There would be no rock 'n' roll without Little Richard. Without rock and roll, there would be no me.

We took a few steps toward the limousine parked on the sidewalk next to us, and the young man tapped the tinted window. It lowered only a few inches, and he leaned in, whispering softly to the person behind the glass. Suddenly, the window rolled down, revealing him in all his magnificence! The hair, the smile, the eyeliner, and the voice that screamed, "God bless you, David!" It's wonderful to meet you!" I was at a loss for words. I stood there like a blathering idiot while he inquired if I was a musician, what my band was called, and where I was from, all while signing a postcard-sized black-and-white portrait of himself with the words, "To David, God cares." We shook hands, the window rolled up, and my life was complete.

I cannot express how important these moments are to me. I wander through this insane life of a musician like a small boy in a museum, surrounded by exhibits that I've spent my entire life studying. And, when I eventually meet someone who has inspired me along the journey, I am grateful. I'm grateful. I don't take any of this for granted. I firmly believe in the shared humanity of music, which I find more satisfying than any other component of my work. When the one-dimensional image transforms into a three-dimensional human being, your spirit is reassured that even our most beloved heroes are made of flesh and bone. I believe that people inspire other people. That is why I feel compelled to connect with my admirers whenever they approach me. I'm a fan, too.

When I was seven years old, my older stoner cousin handed me a copy of Rush's magnum opus, 2112, to take back to Virginia after our annual vacation in Chicago. At this point, I was pretty much stuck to my Beatles and KISS records, so Rush's prog rock musicianship and skill was a whole new universe to my untrained ears. I was intrigued. The drums, however, were the highlight of that CD for me. This was the first time I'd heard them at the forefront of a song, just as lyrical and melodious as the lyrics or guitar. I couldn't play what Neil Peart was playing, but I could feel it.

Decades later, Taylor Hawkins and I were requested to induct Rush into the Rock and Roll Hall of Fame and perform the opening tune on 2112, an instrumental called "Overture" (not an easy task). I'd met bassist Geddy Lee and guitarist Alex Lifeson throughout the years, both incredibly down-to-earth and ridiculously humorous, but never the master himself, Neil Peart. Neil was more mysterious, which is fair given that he was one of the finest drummers of all time (and not just in rock). When Taylor and I arrived for rehearsal the day before the ceremony, Geddy and Alex greeted us, but Neil was not present. And then, in an instant, he emerged and introduced himself in his rich baritone voice: "Hey, Dave, I'm Neil." All I could think was that

He had mentioned my name. He said my name. I cautiously answered hi, and he offered, "Want a coffee?" "Sure!" I said, and we walked over to the catering table, where Neil Peart, Rush's drummer, the man who taught me to hear the drums for the first time at the age of seven and motivated me to become a drummer myself, prepared me a cup of coffee and handed it over with a smile.

INSPIRED YET AGAIN.

It's one thing to see your idols in a musical setting or context; it's another to see them away from the spotlight, in their natural environment, like a wild animal. While I was pushing Violet in a stroller down a busy London shopping street with my wife and our dear friend Dave Koz, Elton John strolled out of a boutique right in front of us and jumped into a waiting car. We all stopped and said, "HOLY SHIT! "Did you just see that?!?!" It was Elton. Fucking. John. And he was star-struck, sitting in a parked car just feet away from where we were standing. My pal nudged me and said, "Go say hi, Dave!" I chuckled and replied, "I don't fucking know Elton John! "And he has no idea who I am!" The automobile began, moved out, drove about twenty meters up the road, and then came to a stop. When the door opened, Elton John sprang out and walked back to us, still frozen in place. He approached me with his wife, toothy grin, saying, "Hello, Dave, nice to meet you." My smile was so big, it practically slid off my face. I introduced him to Jordyn and Dave, and he leaned down to kiss Violet before flying away. Now, THAT is how you do it, I thought. (And, yeah, his massive sapphire earrings complemented his shoes well.)

Years later, I got the opportunity to play drums with Elton on a tune for Queens of the Stone Age's album, Like Clockwork. The song, "Fairweather Friends," was a scorching, unorthodox multipart composition that we meticulously rehearsed before his visit, because Queens' recordings were usually full band live to tape, which meant you had to have your shit together and get it right. Elton arrived, fresh off an Engelbert Humperdinck session (no joke), and remarked, "Okay, boys, what? "Do you have a ballad for me?" We all laughed and said, "No—come listen." For anyone to walk in and learn such a hard song right away was a tall order, but Elton sat at the piano and WORKED on it until he got it perfectly, take after take, ever the perfectionist, proving why he is the queen bitch of rock and roll.

INSPIRED YET AGAIN.

It's the moments with no safety net that keep your spirits up, and if you're an explorer like me, such moments are constantly available. And generally at the most unexpected locations. One night in Osaka, our tour manager, Gus, informed us that Huey Lewis would be attending the show. "HUEY LEWIS!!!" Pat exclaimed. I had never seen him so enthusiastic in all the years I'd known him. Pat once again turned my world upside down when he told me that Huey Lewis and the News' album Sports was one of his favorite recordings of all time (along with Mariah Carey's Butterfly), completely demolishing my idea of him as the punkest motherfucker on the planet. Taylor then informed me that Huey played harmonica on Thin Lizzy's Live and Dangerous record, something I was unaware of but made more sense.

Huey appeared, and the backstage area quickly became alive with our typical pre-show beer and whiskey ritual. Take it from me: Huey is an amazing hang. We drank, smoked, and laughed, and I ultimately inquired about his relationship to Phil Lynott and Thin Lizzy (an incredible band). He told me about his harp solo on that album and how he, too, adored Thin Lizzy. And then I had an idea: what if Huey got up and played a harmonica solo with us? He searched his pockets for a harp, but it was not strapped, though he did declare, "If you can find one in time, I'll do it!" I looked at the clock; we had twenty minutes, so I turned to Gus, begged him to do anything he could to find one, shot one more with Huey, and took the stage. By the seventh song, I looked over and saw Huey beaming and waving his harp in the air. He got out next to me and, with a plastic harmonica purchased on a Sunday night from a Japanese toy store, proceeded to rip a solo that would make the man from Blues Traveler drop his bandoliers and run to his mother. I was completely blown away. This dude is a grade A, all-out badass motherfucker, and I will never question the legitimacy of sports again. Shame on me. For one night only, we were "Huey Lewis and the Foos," and I enjoyed it.

Another twist on an already winding path.

Why are these people so important to me? People inspire people, and over time, they have all become ingrained in my DNA. Every note I've heard them play has had an impact on me. Memories have been painted in my head using their voices as the frame. I recall well when my uncle Tom took me sailing as a child, and we spent the day listening to—you guessed it—"Sailing" by Christopher Cross. If this hadn't been such a formative experience, I might not have confronted a terrified Christopher Cross one day at the Austin, Texas, airport baggage claim, just to catch a look of him in person. Or there was the time I approached Ace Frehley of KISS on a Hollywood street corner at night for a simple handshake, or when I shyly proclaimed my love to Bonnie Raitt on the dressing room floor at the Rock and Roll Hall of Fame. BECAUSE I STILL WALK THROUGH LIFE LIKE A LITTLE BOY IN A MUSEUM, SURROUNDED BY THE EXHIBITS I'VE SPENT MY LIFE STUDYING, AND WHEN I FINALLY COME FACE-TO-FACE WITH SOMETHING OR SOMEONE WHO HAS INSPIRED ME ALONG THE WAY, I AM Grateful. I AM GRATEFUL.

It's one thing to encounter a hero in passing. It's another matter when they become your friend.

Years ago, on a drunken night out with my crew in Los Angeles, I was walking toward the restroom of the seedy bar we were currently destroying when I noticed the one and only Lemmy sitting in the corner, drinking alone in front of a video poker machine (I won't say his last name or band affiliation because if you don't know, I have to break up with you). I couldn't resist. This man was the live, breathing essence of rock & roll, and I had admired him since the first time I heard his gravelly voice roar through my speakers. I approached him and asked, "Excuse me, Lemmy?" I simply wanted to thank you for all the years of inspiration you've provided me." In a dense cloud of Marlboro smoke, he hissed, "Cheers." He glanced up from beneath his black cowboy hat. I was going to turn and walk away when he remarked, "I'm sorry about your friend Kurt."

From that point forward, Lemmy was no longer a globally revered rock and roll deity; he was a fellow human being. And over the years, we became friends, sharing harrowing stories of life on the road and a shared love of Little Richard over thousands of smokes and bottles of Jack Daniel's each time we met. I admired his honesty, candor, and strength, as well as his fragility. Whether bellying up to the bar at the Rainbow Bar and Grill on the Sunset Strip (his home away from home, so much so that once while I was drinking with him there, the waitress came up and delivered him his mail) or at his untidy apartment down the street, I treasured every moment in his company. Because I admired him as a musician and a friend.

The news of his death shocked me. It was just days after his seventieth birthday and only a few weeks since his final show. I assumed he'd outlive us all. He walked a rough route that most people would never survive, and while that way of life took its toll on him later in life, he still had the vigor and spirit of a warrior. Lemmy refused to give up until he had no choice but to rest.

I rushed immediately to a tattoo shop and got an ace of spades and the words "SHAKE YOUR BLOOD," a phrase from a song we wrote together years ago, tattooed on my left wrist. He was a passionate rock and roll fan who lived life to the fullest, two things we definitely had in common.

A week or two later, I was invited to speak at his memorial service, and while holding back tears, I told a few memories about our time together in front of the small church full of his oldest friends. This was a bittersweet celebration of his life, because he had brought us all so much joy while leaving us to face life without his invaluable friendship.

Pulling the small black-and-white picture that Little Richard had autographed for me years ago from my jacket pocket, I stood and read the lyrics of an old gospel hymn that Little Richard once sung, "Precious Lord, Take My Hand."

Precious Lord, take my hand

Lead me on, let me stand

I am tired, I am weak, I am worn

Through the storm, through the night

Lead me on to the light

Take my hand, precious Lord

Lead me home

I turned around and placed the image on Lemmy's altar as a thank you.

Forever grateful for the inspiration.

PART 5

LIVING

BEDTIME STORIES WITH JOAN JETT

"Hey, Harper . . . hey, Violet . . . what's goin' on?"

My two kids sat in startled silence as Joan Jett, the one and only Queen of Rock and Roll, stood at the foot of the couch. With her spiky black hair, old Converse Chucks, and tight jean jacket, she threw a deep shadow over their cherubic faces like a warrior statue, her typical gravelly voice rising above the sound of afternoon cartoons in the background. "Guys! "This is JOAN JETT!" I exclaimed, hoping for some form of response. I could see their little thoughts racing, urgently attempting to absorb this bizarre encounter, but they were rendered speechless. I had already informed Joan on the way over to the house that this would happen, saying that my daughters were very familiar with her... they had just never met a superhero in person.

A few months prior, during a European tour, I had decided to take my daughters to the massive London department store Harrods on a wet day off for some rug-rat retail therapy. It was too cold for the park and too rainy for a walk, so I decided to take them on a tour of its famed toy department, which dwarfed most American toy stores, so they could get out of the hotel and have some fun. I know that it is not as culturally gratifying as visiting one of the city's many beautiful museums, but sometimes you simply have to say "Fuck it" and give the people what they want. Especially when the people are less than four feet tall. As enjoyable as exploring the world with your family can be, keeping youngsters from becoming stir-crazy Moving from one hotel room to the next becomes a mission over time, and you find yourself continuously researching activities days in advance to avoid becoming trapped in a vicious loop of room service chicken fingers and subtitled cartoons. Even after a night of thrashing my body in blazing loudness, I've always tried to turn these moments of chance into adventure, transforming an otherwise weary tour into a frenetic rock and roll family vacation. Over the years, I've been fortunate to show them the globe, from the canals of Venice, Italy, to Sydney Harbour, from Iceland's glaciers to the Eiffel Tower, and everything in between. Along the way, I've joyfully watched my children progress from car seats strapped into airplanes and bassinets next to hotel beds to waving down flight attendants for more ginger ale and ordering room service ice cream sundaes alone at midnight. They are now seasoned travelers, which I adore since it means we can stay together.

As the trip progressed, we made our way to New York City for a performance at Madison Square Garden, one of my favorite venues in the world. The drive into the building always reminded me of a scene from Led Zeppelin's live concert video The Song Remains the Same, which I practically studied as a teenager, attempting to deconstruct John Bonham's superhuman drumming skills. On our drive to the city, our tour manager, Gus, asked if we wanted to invite any special visitors to join us for the show. After all, it was Madison Square Garden, and we needed to make it a memorable occasion. Names were thrown about the vehicle, largely of friends we'd jammed with before, until someone mentioned Joan Jett, who had lived in the city since the late 1970s. Having never met her previously, I inquired about how we could contact her. Gus responded with, "Pat knows her!"

Pat Smear, our founding guitarist and reigning minister of cool, knew Joan from his days with the iconic band the Germs. Pat, who was born and raised in Los Angeles, was a punk rock kid in the mid-

1970s and a major fan of Joan's first band, the Runaways, an all-girl group raised on Bowie and T-Rex music. He had seen all of their gigs and finally became friends with Joan, running in a pack of Hollywood punks who, unknowingly, would influence the course of music for good.

Pat, who was roughly the same age as Joan, was so inspired by the Runaways, who were all still teenagers at the time, that he and his best buddy, Darby Crash, decided to form their own band. And when it came time to record their first full-length studio album, GI, in 1979, they recruited Joan Jett to produce. So there was a rich history there, not just in the annals of rock and roll, but also personally.

After a few phone calls, we learned that Joan would be delighted to make an appearance, so we quickly scheduled for her to come down and run through her legendary song "Bad Reputation" with us before the event. It was an excellent choice for our audience because Joan was one of our generation's most recognized singers and would definitely top off the historic evening with a boom. As we drove into the arena in a motorcade, much as Led Zeppelin had thirty-eight years previously, I was filled with excitement, pinching myself for the chance to meet another idol, a fierce woman who set her own rules.

When Joan arrived through the changing room door, I stood up in nervous excitement and raced over to greet her. I was now face to face with the genuine Joan Jett. That black, spiky hair, those ancient Converse Chucks, and that tight jacket were no longer just images on a television screen, nor was that gravelly voice merely a sound from an old speaker. She had a powerful presence, as tough and punk as ever. And, my gosh, she smelled fantastic.

We practiced the song on practice instruments in our dressing rooms before putting it at the conclusion of the set list, knowing it would undoubtedly be the show's highlight. Joan was a joy to be around, her murderous scowl replaced by a smile that could have lit up Madison Square Garden on its own, and it thrilled my heart to see her and Pat reunited after all these years. Without these two, who knows where we'd be? I felt like an extra in a documentary that I'd gladly pay money to see.

By the way, do not underestimate Joan's presence. Before the show, I was standing in a crowded corridor, catching up with old friends over cocktails, when Joan discreetly emerged from our dressing room. As she slowly strolled down the corridor alone, like a post-apocalyptic James Dean, I saw every solitary person, men and women alike, hug the walls, astonished by her presence. She sliced a way through the audience one stride at a time, inspiring a collective swoon rivaled only by Elvis. This was freaking rock & roll. Joan was truly a superhero.

When I introduced her onstage that night, I noticed that she had this effect on almost everyone. The crowd roared as she went into the spotlight, a thunderous greeting fit for a legend, and our performance was tight, rapid, and spot-on. Afterward, we toasted with a bottle of champagne, and Joan and I discussed working together someday. "We should write some songs together!" she suggested with her loud New York accent. I excitedly agreed, and we compared schedules right away, successfully finding a time when we were both off the road to meet and record. We agreed on a date and hugged warmly, happy for the chance encounter and looking forward to the next.

I couldn't wait to inform my girls that their favorite superhero was not only visiting Los Angeles to write with me, but would also be staying with us for the weekend. Their minds would be blown!

When the illusion of toys and YouTube videos becomes a reality, it is difficult for a child to fully appreciate breaking the fourth wall. Violet was just five, and Harper was two years old. Nonetheless, I did my best to prepare them for Joan's coming, hoping that it wouldn't plunge them into an existential crisis. I mean, if SpongeBob SquarePants showed up at your front door, I'm sure you'd be surprised, too.

According to their reaction on the couch that day, our brief before pep talk had not made much of an impact.

"Okay, gentlemen. Do you remember the Barbie I bought in London? She is coming to stay with us this weekend."

Crickets.

"So, when she gets here . . . don't freak out . . . she's real."

More crickets.

After we settled in, Joan and I went to the Foo Fighters' studio and started working on a song idea she had called "Any Weather," an up-tempo track with one of her signature melodies. It was immediately recognizable as Joan Jett, full of attitude and heart. Watching her work, I could only imagine what a great life she had led, and I could sense her unwavering love of rock and roll, which was both contagious and inspiring. Even after all these years, she continued to sing from her heart.

That night, after a tremendously busy day, we returned home, and I began my regular ritual of getting my girls ready for bed, while Joan went to the guesthouse to change into her pajamas. I gave Harper a bath, changed her into PJs, read her a couple stories, and put her in her cot without a sound. One down; one to go. Violet was next. Bath and PJs, but before she went to bed, I walked her down to the living room to say goodbye to Joan.

I stood in front of the couch, where Joan was sitting comfortably in her own jammies, and said, "Hey, Joan, Violet wanted to say good night to you." Joan smiled and said, "Awwwwww, good night Violet. "I will see you tomorrow!" Violet turned towards me and whispered in my ear, "Dad, will you ask Joan if she'll read me bedtime stories tonight?" My heart stopped for a second as I peered into Violet's eyes, and then I turned to Joan. "Hey . . . ummmm . . . she wants you to read her bedtime stories tonight . . ." Violet's grip tightened in suspense. Joan grinned and gladly cooperated. "Come on, Violet . . . let's go!"

As I watched the two walk hand in hand upstairs, I prayed that Violet would never forget this moment, that she would one day reflect back on this night and realize that some superheroes do exist. Maybe someday she'll be her own type of innovator, an architect, a pioneer, motivating generations of young ladies to pick up a guitar or do whatever she wants to do to make her imprint.

IN A WORLD FULL OF BARBIES, EVERY GIRL NEEDS A JOAN JETT.

THE DADDY-DAUGHTER DANCE

"Oh, by the way. ..This year's daddy-daughter dance will take place on March sixth. Make sure you add it to your calendar."

My heart stopped as my wife's voice resonated through the exaggerated delay of a long-distance call from Los Angeles to my hotel room in Cape Town, South Africa. Is it March sixth? I thought to myself. Oh, please make that a day off at home. ..I knew right away that this was going to be a problem, but I tried to hide the sinking feeling in my chest as I casually told Jordyn that I'd make a note of it, hung up the phone, and broke out in a nervous sweat, praying that this most important date (an event I had promised I'd never miss) fell during one of our never-ending world tour breaks that year. Fearing the worst, I dashed across the room to my laptop and promptly opened my calendar to March 6.

Okay, it was a show day. ..in Perth, Australia.

Violet's school had a daddy-daughter dance ritual that was essentially required for any parent trying to raise a girl in Los Angeles' Silicon Valley (no, I'm not referring to software). An opportunity to deepen the family tie, spend quality time together, and demonstrate that no matter what, a daughter can always rely on her loving old father. From kindergarten to sixth grade, it was an annual parade of middle-aged men trying to politely socialize with one another in their starched business suits, while their little girls, dressed in miniature ball gowns with corsages carefully pinned, ate candy hand over fist from long tables that would make Willy Wonka blush. All set to a Kidz Bop, Top 40 soundtrack DJ'd by a Nickelodeon-style dance teacher screaming "cha-cha slide" directions at ear-shattering volume. It was usually hosted in one of the dismal banquet rooms of the famed Sportsmen's Lodge in Sherman Oaks (home of a thousand Bar Mitzvahs), and it was the pinnacle of most little girls' lives. There are also a few fathers.

Violet and I always made a big deal out of it. Though I've always disliked formal clothing (because I look like a stoner in court to pay a misdemeanor marijuana fine), I'd go to great lengths to clean up and look the part. Violet, of course, would do her Disney best, generally dressed as a princess in a tricky pair of small heels, bursting with delight but yet terrified at the idea of such an embarrassing social experiment. Deep down, I realized that these formative rituals would undoubtedly serve as the foundation for many future high school dances, therefore it was critical that they go successfully for my daughter; otherwise, she may face an adolescence of proms matching Carrie's bucket-of-blood incident.

This year was different, however. Harper, who is three years younger than Violet, would usually stand wailing at the door when Violet and I left for the dance, pleading to be included despite the fact that she was not yet a student at the school. It crushed my heart to see her wave goodbye while holding back tears with her pacifier, unable to comprehend her ineligibility. I'd always comfort her, "We'll all go together someday!"" Nonetheless, the image of her standing at the doorway, tears flowing down her cheeks, clutching her beloved blanket, always hits me right where it hurts. And now that she was old enough and I had the opportunity to follow through on my promise to take them both to the dance, which Harper had been looking forward to for nearly half her life, I had a fucking gig the same night—9,330 miles away.

I immediately called my 30-year manager, John Silva, and told him, "John, we have a problem. Like, a big problem." I gently stated the scenario in my most measured tone, emphasizing that missing the dance was not an option. He apologized, "I'm sorry, David, but the show's already sold out." DEFCON 1 kicked in as I visualized the horror of my two tiny children being stood up at the dance by THEIR OWN FATHER, and I suddenly went from zero to sixty, yelling, "Cancel it!" Move it! Postpone it! Do whatever it takes, but I can't and won't miss this fucking dance!"

Recognizing the gravity of this possible tragedy, we put our thinking caps on and began rearranging dates. I mean, if they could send a man to the moon, they could certainly get me to the Sportsmen's Lodge on time in my Levi's and muddy Clarks shoes, right? The tour, which began in Christchurch, New Zealand, was relatively brief, consisting of eight stadium events in the blazing summer heat. It was going to be our biggest trip down under yet, and tickets sold out immediately. We have always had a passionate love affair with our friends in New Zealand and Australia, making it a point to visit at least once every album cycle, despite the fifteen-hour journey time. And it's always well worth it. From the black pebble beaches of Piha, New Zealand, just outside of the cosmopolitan wonderland of Auckland, to the wineries that surround the hills of Adelaide, Australia, we had spent a decade exploring this heavenly territory, making lifelong friends and rocking the fuck out of every venue we set foot in. It hurt me to even consider postponing, let alone canceling, a show. Plus, disappointing fans is simply not in my DNA. But, as much as I enjoy a nice, cold Victoria Bitter beer and a pork pie at midnight, I still have priorities. After some brainstorming/shuffling and a few phone calls, we devised a plan:

The Perth show, which was already sold out, could be moved from the sixth to the eighth, giving me just enough time to run offstage in Adelaide, board a chartered plane to Sydney, immediately jump on a Qantas flight back to L.A., land at LAX, sleep a few hours, take my girls to the dance, then leave straight from the Sportsmen's Lodge for the airport and fly back to Perth just in time to run onstage and kick their fucking asses.

CRAZY? Possibly doable. BARELY. MANDATORY? INDISPUTABLY.

Our plan was set in motion, and the lovely folks of Perth graciously changed their schedules so that we could meet on March 8. Crisis averted. I could finally relax knowing that I would be there for my daughters, escorting them in my best Levi's and Clarks shoes and telling them that they could always count on their father, even if it meant forty hours of travel over two days and sixteen time zones. Fortunately, all of those years spent stuffed in dirty, crowded vehicles for months on end, sleeping on floors and subsisting on corn dogs had prepared me for this precise moment. You do whatever you need to do to get to the gig. Always.

By the time we arrived in Adelaide, our transcontinental operation had been planned down to the minute with military precision. Leaving no space for error or delay, my tour manager, Gus, and I were ready to jump from the stage like soldiers from a Black Hawk helicopter and dash to a private plane waiting for us on a nearby tarmac, where we would be flown to Sydney to connect for the exhausting fifteen-hour flight home. To say the least, it was a daunting task, but one that we both looked forward to, chuckling at the silliness of it all. The show that night was a ripper, a twenty-four-song blitz that had the stadium going crazy while I kept a tight eye on the clock on the side of the stage, making sure I gave the audience every last second of my time before I had to go. As the final chords of "Everlong" hung in the air, Gus and I hopped into a car and drove to a small local airport, where we planned to circle the earth together.

When I arrived in Los Angeles, I looked like I'd been struck by a garbage truck, but as soon as I went through the main door, I was greeted by two wailing small girls, a feeling that outlasted even the most severe jet lag. Knowing I only had a few hours with them, I suppressed any physical tiredness and went into "dad mode". Full disclosure: I am what some people could consider a stupid parent (shocking, I know); I frequently resemble one of those incredibly annoying kids' television show hosts who make you want to put your head in an oven. I am not opposed to embarrassing myself for the slightest giggle from my children, from the moment they wake up until bedtime stories at night. For example, I've always found that dancing like a fool to Earth, Wind, and Fire while serving pancakes in the morning not only evokes the first smile of the day, but also sends them out the front door with a skip in their step, even if it's only to escape my insane behavior.

The rest of the day was spent sipping copious amounts of coffee and trying to keep my eyes from slamming shut while planning the evening's activities. Stretch limousine? Check. Is there fake champagne? Check. Failed attempt to appear formal after an almost ten-thousand-mile commute. Do a double check. This was their big night, so the pageantry and preparation were nothing short of Oscar-worthy, complete with a glam squad that could easily pass for a NASCAR pit crew. Violet was an experienced daddy-daughter dancer by this point, but Harper's eyes told me that this was something special. She'd been waiting for this moment for a long time. And it was worth every mile I had traveled.

As we entered the main area, we were greeted with the usual balloons, tables perfectly set with gorgeous dishes, a magnificent buffet of boring spaghetti and chicken nuggets, and a dance floor filled with screaming youngsters. Our eyes glowed like Dorothy's as she entered the magical world of Oz, and we exchanged a group hug as we assessed the scene. What do I do first? Eat? Dance? Attack the cotton candy machine? Expecting Violet and Harper to be nervous, I suggested, "How about we locate a table and set our things down?" I turned to see an empty seat, and. ..They dashed toward their companions, shrieking with delight as they danced in small groups. I could only grin as I watched them share their excitement with the rest of the girls. My job here was finished, and I was left to socialize with a roomful of similarly abandoned fathers, passing the time with stiff-as-starch chats about sports, which I knew nothing about. If fatherhood has taught me anything, it's that I couldn't pick a Hall of Fame athlete out of a lineup if my life depended on it. To be honest, I enjoy being the guy at the party who is always more interested in the Super Bowl halftime show than the game itself.

Gus and I boarded the plane, and I emptied my exhausted bones into the large seat, passing off in a lovely red-wine haze before we even left the ground. Mission completed.

Turbulence. Not the kind that feels like a massage chair in a mall. No. The sort that feels like a 9.0 earthquake, flinging you around like a feather in the wind (thank you, Robert Plant), while also jarring your organs and scaring you to death. It will pass, I told myself. I got this. After about twenty minutes, I felt a piercing pain in my stomach, like if someone had taken a knife and carved their initials into my intestines, like lovers do on park benches and old oak trees. This wasn't usual. This wasn't motion sickness. It was food poisoning. As the plane violently swayed back and forth, I realized I was now imprisoned in this aluminum tube with thirteen hours to go, and every abrupt movement made me want to...explode. I broke out in a cold sweat, looking at the seat belt light, wishing for it to turn off so I could go to the bathroom and get rid of these pollutants, but the turbulence lasted what seemed like a lifetime.

Food illness is every touring musician's worst nightmare. When you have a cold, you consume hot tea. If you have the flu, you take medication. If you get food poisoning, you are completely fucked. There is no way to prevent your body from doing what it is genetically programmed to do: puke and spit poison out of you. However, I have a larger dilemma. I'm physically incapable of vomiting. I may have thrown up three times since the age of twelve: once at fourteen while listening to David Bowie's "Space Oddity" outside of a keg party (nothing worse than heaving up still-cold Meister Brau), once in 1997 after a bad piece of street pizza in Hollywood (seemed like a good idea at the time), and once in 2011 after seeing Soundgarden at the Los Angeles Forum (it wasn't the music, I assure you). So any bout of sickness is usually a protracted process of convincing myself that I can handle it. Basically, this is my hell.

The seat belt light eventually turned off, and I was in the bathroom in seconds, shutting the door and leaning over the sink while I attempted to relax and let nature take its course. As the minutes passed, I became increasingly aware that not only was this attempt to expel my inner demons futile, but I was most likely raising the suspicions of every passenger and flight attendant in the cabin by "overstaying my welcome" in this tiny lavatory. After a good collegiate try, I stumbled back to my seat and burst out in chills. I looked at the clock. ..There are twelve hours to go.

The subsequent flight was a nightmare. Multiple trips to the restroom resulted in futile attempts, and I returned to my seat for another round of spasmodic chills and fever. No sleep. There's no rest. Just an ongoing worst-case scenario that couldn't have happened at a more inconvenient time, given that I had to head directly to the gig for soundcheck upon arriving in Perth. I thought this was a test. A test of will, devotion, and the age-old adage "You do what you have to do to get to the gig."

Ebola was currently making headlines. The horrible disease was causing shock waves of fear all around the world, and international travel was fraught with precautionary procedures that required all passengers to be vetted in some fashion. As we approached Sydney, I was given the standard customs and immigration cards to complete, but there was also a required Ebola questionnaire that everyone had to sign. A basic yes-or-no form with a list of symptoms that indicate you might have Ebola. I read the list with horror. Nausea. Diarrhea. Fever. Feeling the chills. ..I was displaying each one of them. My mind raced ahead to being thrown in a room full of people with true Ebola at the airport, where I would get the disease and eventually die alone in the land Down Under. I sat up in my chair, put on my best game face, and attempted to will my illness away.

I stood up, drained of energy, as we disembarked the plane and muttered to Gus, "Dude, I have food poisoning." His eyes widened, and we held our stars as the plane door opened. We still had a five-hour trip to Perth. This wasn't done; it had only just started. like we walked to baggage claim, he took out his phone and began scrambling to figure out how to fix this most awful scenario, just like he usually did. Our master plan had been derailed, all bets were off, and it had turned into a rock-and-roll version of The Amazing Race. What appeared to be a ludicrous adventure at first became a simple survival challenge. All in the name of the Father.

By the time we boarded the following flight, Gus had arranged for a doctor to meet me at the Perth hotel. Fortunately, it appeared like the worst was gone, and it was now just a matter of trying to keep down some tea and toast, hoping that it would supply even the smallest sliver of the stamina that I would require to pull off another two-and-a-half-hour screaming rock concert. That seemed like an insurmountable assignment, but there was no turning back now. The stage was prepared, the gear was ready, and thousands of devoted Food fans were gearing up for the night of their lives.

As I circled the planet for the final time, I reflected on my connection with my father and wondered if he would have done the same for me. Would he have gone to any length to be there for me on such a momentous occasion? Doubtful, I thought. Perhaps I love so passionately as a parent because mine cannot.

I absolutely believe that your interpretation or "version" of love is acquired by example from the start, and it serves as your divining rod throughout life, for better or ill. A basis for all meaningful relationships to build on. My mother has undoubtedly contributed to my success. I love my children as much as I was loved as a child, and I hope they will do the same when the time comes. Some cycles are meant to be broken, while others are meant to be reinforced.

Years later, I was taking Harper to school when she said, "Dad, what is the longest flight you've ever taken?" I grinned and said, "Okay. ..Remember when I returned home for one night to take you to your first father-daughter dance?" She nodded. "That was about twenty hours in the air," that's what I said. She looked at me like I was insane. "Twenty hours???" You didn't need to do that!!!"

We exchanged smiles, and after a long moment, she turned to face me and said, "Actually... Yes, you did."

THE WISDOM OF VIOLET

"Are you sitting down?"

John Silva's voice, fatally hoarse from decades of yelling commands from his cluttered Hollywood office, could not have been clearer at this moment. After all, no one wants to hear these four words at the beginning of a phone conversation, especially from the man in control of their career. "Yes . . . why, what is it???" I instantly yelled back, expecting some dreadful news as shock waves of fear and worry flooded every vein in my body.

"Academy Awards called. They want you to sing 'Blackbird' solo at the concert this year."

I paused in my tracks, and my thoughts immediately went to the moment when all eyes and cameras would be on me, alone with only an acoustic guitar, live on television in front of thirty-four million people. Even though I was wearing sweatpants in my home room and the show was weeks away, debilitating stage fear struck me immediately. I couldn't imagine a more scary scenario. I could only voice a hushed "Holy shit!" in answer.

I was familiar with the song, of course. The arrangement had been imprinted on my memory since I was a child, and I ultimately learnt Paul McCartney's sophisticated fingerpicking guitar style while singing along to his timeless melody. However, it is one thing to smoothly perform such a challenging song from the comfort of your own home. It's another thing entirely to do it in front of the entire planet (not to mention Jennifer Lawrence and Sylvester Stallone).

With the phone nearly slipping from my already moist palm, I croaked back, "Wait... why?" It made very little sense to me. The band was on sabbatical (or, as we call it, "I hate us") at the time, and I certainly hadn't been nominated for an Oscar, so why would they call me? "They would like you to be the musical accompaniment for the 'In Memoriam' segment," Silva said. Not the most encouraging opportunity, I thought, but having never been one to back down from a challenge, I said, "Let me sleep on it, and I'll call you tomorrow."

I hung up the phone and sat in silence, my mind racing back and forth between every reason to take this unique chance and every excuse to politely decline. The invitation to pay respect to individuals who had passed away in the film industry that year was an enormous honor, but... I wondered if I could pull it off. Deep down, I was afraid. After all, "Blackbird" is hardly a stroll in the park, and performing at the Oscars is not the same as performing in front of a packed arena of Foo fans.

Fortunately, I had already played the song, albeit to a totally different audience.

That would have been Violet's third-grade Student Entertainment Day the previous year.

Student Entertainment Day, no longer referred to as a talent show due to concerns about the long-term psychological impact of competition on our next generation of children (cue exaggerated eye roll), was typically a cavalcade of children performing piano recitals or lip-syncing along to Katy Perry songs with intricately choreographed dance routines for a gymnasium full of helicopter parents dressed in Lululemon activewear.

When it was announced that year, Violet dashed home and excitedly requested if she could play "Sgt. Pepper's Lonely Hearts Club Band" with her closest pals. Not an unusual request by her standards, as I had made it a point to indoctrinate her with the Beatles' whole repertoire from a young age, aiming to create some sort of solid musical foundation before she went on to Cardi B and Iggy Azalea. I could tell from her enthusiasm that she was thrilled to finally have the opportunity to share her undeniable talent with others, something I had been looking forward to since the first time I heard her beautiful voice singing along to Amy Winehouse songs from her little car seat on long drives through the San Fernando Valley. A few phone calls were made to test the waters, but to our dismay, the prevailing consensus among her dearest friends was, "Sgt. who?"

Violet was upset when she learned that her pals would not be joining her for the event. As we sat on the couch together, and I watched the tears fall down her cherubic little face, the protective father in me stepped in. "Hey, how about you and I perform 'Blackbird' together?" "I'll play guitar, and you sing!" She looked up and wiped her cheeks, and her expression immediately turned to one of excitement and relief. I dashed to get my guitar, sat down in front of her, and began to play the song. Without a rehearsal or lyric sheet to refer to, she arrived on time and in tune, and we played it wonderfully on the first try. It was beautiful. I would say I was surprised, but I was not. I knew she could do it. But, could I? We exchanged high-fives and devised a plan: we'd rehearse every morning before school and every night before bed until the gig, ensuring that we'd be completely prepared by the time we took the stage.

Saturday Night Live, Wembley Stadium, and the White House—each of these momentous performances was a career highlight, but my nervousness about them was nothing compared to how apprehensive I was for this occasion. I didn't mind that it was just a gymnasium full of parents sipping iced nonfat lattes and fingering their smartphones. I was there for Violet, and it was critical that the performance went smoothly. So, from that day forward, I spent every spare time practicing to be her impeccable musical accompaniment, perfecting that exquisite guitar arrangement until I had blisters on every finger. THIS IS THE MOST IMPORTANT GIG OF MY LIFE, I BELIEVE.

We arrived for soundcheck the morning before the event, beautifully dressed and well-prepared. I asked for a stool to sit on while playing. Violet requested a music stand for her lyrics on the unusual occasion that she required them. We tested the guitar and microphone levels before nervously waiting for the room to fill up. Violet, who had been at this school since kindergarten, knew almost everyone, but her great singing talent had been kept hidden, and it was about to be revealed to this most unsuspecting audience.

After a few adorable performances, our names were called, and we climbed the stage to a smattering of cheers. We took our seats and sank in the dreadful pin-drop silence. "Ready, Boo?" I asked Violet. She nodded nervously, and I began the gentle guitar opening, reminding myself that this was, without a doubt, the most significant performance of both my and her lives. As always, she arrived perfectly on time and in tune, and I watched the audience's jaws drop. Her innocent, crystalline voice filled the PA, leaving the gathering awestruck. I could only smile when they finally met the Violet I knew so well. As the final chord struck, we were greeted with loud applause and a standing ovation. We took a bow, high-fived, and passed the stage to the next performer. "You nailed it, Boo!" I said this while hugging her.

My heart felt full of pride. Violet is proud not only of her musical ability, but also of her courage.

Courage is a defining characteristic in the life of any artist. The courage to express your deepest emotions, to show your true voice, or to stand in front of an audience and lay it all out for the world to see. The emotional sensitivity required to summon a great song can also work against you when you share it with the world. This is a crippling conflict for any sensitive artist. A feeling I've had with every lyric I've performed for someone other than myself. Will they enjoy it? Am I good enough? The bravery to be yourself is what brings those competing emotions together, and when it does, magic happens.

Still undecided about the Academy Awards, I waited for Violet to return home from school before informing her. After much deliberation, I decided to decline, rationalizing myself that I didn't need to play the Oscars and that I'd probably botch everything up anyway, but I thought I'd share the insanity of the offer with my daughter. As she came bouncing through the door with her backpack full of books, I said, "Guess what I got asked to do today!" "What?" she inquired. "To play 'Blackbird' at the Academy Awards!" She stared me dead in the eyes and asked, "Well? You're going to do it, right? I mean, you did it during Student Entertainment Day!"

The gauntlet was thrown. In an instant, I realized I needed to play the Oscars. As her father, I now had to demonstrate to her that I possessed the same fortitude that she had mustered in the gymnasium that day, no matter how afraid I was. Of course, I had to prove to her that I was capable, but I also had to prove it to myself.

I called John Silva, accepted the offer, and started preparing for the biggest performance of my life.

It was decided that I would perform the song with an orchestra as a montage of images was presented above me. But there was a catch: the song had been completely altered to fit the sequence of photos, and the orchestra was to be piped in from a studio down the street, leaving me alone on stage with no conductor to refer to if I needed assistance following the rapidly fluctuating speed. As a result, I had to play to a "click track" via an ear monitor, which would serve as a metronome reference. Easy enough, right? Fun fact: I have never used or played with in-ear monitors. I still prefer old-school floor monitors that resemble dusty old speakers and blow your hair back with each kick drum hit. So this was a significant issue. How was I going to pull this off without a conductor to watch or a track to click on?

I ultimately gave in and unwillingly consented to use an in-ear monitor for the first time in my life, in front of thirty-four million people. What did I get myself into? I thought. In the event of a trainwreck-level emergency, I planned to simply find Jennifer Lawrence in the front row and serenade her as best I could. Sylvester Stallone might suffice in a pinch.

The Academy Awards are the pinnacle of award events. You nearly need Pentagon entrance clearance just to plug in your instrument, and the procedure of being "dressed" is straight out of Cinderella. Not my feelings. I'm used to walking into an event after a few cocktails wearing a blazer that's appropriate for both funerals and court hearings. But this was different. I was immediately granted an appointment at a Beverly Hills boutique to be fitted for the perfect suit. To put it mildly, I felt out of place.

Standing in front of the clothing racks, I had no idea where to begin. Anyone who knows me knows that I am the least trendy person on the planet, and I still dress like I did in ninth grade (Vans, jeans, band T-shirt), so I was assigned a stylist to help me choose and fit the right suit. I was shortly introduced to Kelsey, a stylish young blond woman with huge blue eyes. "We've actually met before," she explained. I stared at her face and, while it appeared familiar, I couldn't identify the memory. "I was the little girl in Nirvana's 'Heart-Shaped Box' video . . ." Silence, as she puts it. Then I noticed it in those large, blue eyes. That was her.

Mind. Fucking. Blown. THE UNIVERSE WAS HARD AT WORK.

That video, shot twenty-three years ago and directed by famed photographer Anton Corbijn, was a surrealist mosaic of birth, death, anatomy, and chaos set in a fantasy world, with an elderly man hanging on a cross in a Jesus Christ posture. Standing in the midst of it all was a tiny girl dressed in a white hood and robe, her huge eyes filled with melancholy, possibly representing Nirvana's innocence lost throughout our horrific ascent to popularity. And now we were reunited in a fitting room, fastening the cuffs of the jeans I'd be wearing while playing a Beatles song in front of a room full of movie stars. Irony, anyone?

As the date approached, I got increasingly worried. When I had dinner with Paul McCartney a week before the Oscars, I told him I would be performing on the show. "What song will you be playing?" Paul questioned me. "'Blackbird,'" I anxiously responded. "Cheeky," he replied, smiling and wagging his finger at me. Funny, but that added to the pressure, as I now had another motive not to screw things up.

I would repeatedly return to the vision of Violet onstage, demonstrating to herself that she had the bravery to bare her innermost sentiments, disclose her genuine voice, and stand in front of an audience, laying it all out there for the world to see. I was inspired by her fortitude, so I discovered my own and dedicated my performance to her in my heart.

Take it from me: watching the Oscars from your living room with some spinach dip and a frosty Coors Light is far more pleasurable than attending. I admire anyone who gives their lives to the arts, but it felt like the longest Catholic Mass you could ever imagine, minus the crackers and thimbles of wine. And my performance was near the end of the program, leaving me with mounting anxiety. Hours have passed. Days. Weeks. After what felt like an eternity, I was eventually summoned backstage to prepare.

During a commercial break, I strolled out to my chair in the middle of the stage and gazed down at the front row, where Jennifer Lawrence and Sylvester Stallone had been sitting all night, hoping to see their faces to save me if I choked up and my performance went wrong. They were nowhere to be found, replaced by seat fillers who all looked at me with puzzled expressions, apparently anticipating Lady Gaga. "One minute!" a director exclaimed over the PA. I inserted my small ear monitor, adjusted the microphone, took a big breath, and closed my eyes.

I saw Violet. I witnessed her first steps as a baby. I saw her on her first day of school, waving farewell from a distance. I witnessed her pedaling away on a bicycle for the first time, no longer requiring the help of her adoring father. And I witnessed her perform "Blackbird" in the school gymnasium. I FELT HER COURAGE AND FOUND MINE.

Unfortunately, Jennifer and Sly missed it.

CONCLUSION: ANOTHER STEP IN THE CROSSWALK

"Are you okay, buddy?""

Slumped over in my chair, I gave Chris a silent, reassuring nod before hiding my face in a dirty backstage towel and crying, my muffled cries echoing in the awkward silence of our dressing room as the other guys quietly opened their wardrobe cases and changed their clothes behind me, still sweating from the three-hour show we had just performed. After twenty years in a band, Pat, Nate, Taylor, Chris, and Rami had never seen me, their strong leader, fully break down in front of them. But I couldn't keep it all in anymore. I needed to let go. In a moment of catharsis, it was as if every feeling I had suppressed for the previous forty years rose to the surface and finally breached the levee inside of me, overflowing into the concrete floor beneath.

It wasn't that I couldn't walk but had gone on an exhaustive tour of sixty-five shows where I had to be put onto a chair each night to act, only to be hauled away like a broken stage prop. It wasn't that I still felt the excruciating pain of the jagged titanium screws bored deep into my bones, which will serve as a constant reminder of my weakness and fragility. And it wasn't that I was overwhelmed with the awful need for my family that tears my heart when we're separated for weeks at a time, preying on my fear of absence and my father's separation anxiety.

No, it was something different.

It was the fact that I had just finished playing a sold-out gig to 40,000 people at Chicago's Wrigley Field, exactly across the street from the Cubby Bear, the tiny club where I watched my first concert when I was thirteen years old and was motivated to commit my life to rock and roll.

I'd played stadiums twice the size previously, leading a sea of fans in chorus after chorus for hours in thrilling unison, but it wasn't the sheer vastness of the place that moved me to tears that night. It was the fact that Wrigley Field was only a crosswalk away from that dimly illuminated corner tavern formerly full with bodies writhing and dancing to the thunderous shriek of feedback and smashing drums that acted as my awakening. That July night in 1982, when my cousin Tracey took me to see Naked Raygun, it was like a baptism; I was immersed in the distorted grandeur of music. From that day on, I was transformed, empowered by the revelation that occurred as my scrawny little chest was pressed against the tiny stage and I was confronted with the raw power of rock and roll. I'd finally discovered my specialty, tribe, and calling. But most importantly, I'd discovered myself.

This was my profound awakening, and my dreams were no longer just that; they had become my divining rod. I was an idealistic misfit, fueled by the audacity of faith and a reckless drive to do things on my own. Punk rock became my professor in a school with no rules, teaching me that no lectures are necessary and that everyone has a voice that deserves to be heard, regardless of the sound. I've formed my life on this idea and blindly pursued it with unwavering belief.

That night, I stepped out onto the crosswalk, and there was no turning back.

As the band quietly filed out of the dressing room, I was left alone in my chair to contemplate and gradually reassemble the jagged parts of this lifelong puzzle. I recalled the long trips my mother and I would take in our old 1976 Ford Maverick sedan, singing along to AM radio, when I first heard the sound of two voices in harmony producing a chord. This was the spark that kindled my passion for music. I remembered the wonderful instrumental ferocity of Edgar Winter's "Frankenstein," my first album, bought at the drugstore and played on the record player my mother brought home from school until the old needle wore out. I remembered the Silvertone guitar with the amp built into the case, which I used to play every day after school, strumming along to Beatles songs and learning about the beauty of songwriting and arrangement. And I remembered the old pillows I used as drums on my bedroom floor, thrashing along to my favorite punk rock recordings until my hands were bloodied.

Each tear triggers a recollection. Each recollection represents another step in the crosswalk.

Perhaps my séance worked after all. It had been thirty years since I petitioned the cosmos for this blessing, as I knelt before the flickering candles of the shrine I'd built in my carport. Maybe it was just a matter of expressing desire and believing that everything is attainable if you put your mind to it completely. Perhaps it was the courage of believing in oneself. Perhaps I'd sold my soul. All of this could be true, but I knew that if it hadn't been for the insight I had that night at the Cubby Bear, I would never have tried.

I would never have taken the opportunity and called to audition for my favorite local band, Scream, kicking off a chain of events that would change my life forever. If I hadn't seen that flier on the bulletin board at my local music store, I would have taken a completely different path, but I saw a door open before me, and rather than staying in the comfort of my tiny bedroom, I decided to dive through it, leaving a life of stability and security behind. Despite remaining linked to my youth, I was eager to be free. I was willing to risk everything on the fiery desire that blazed within me, and I promised to honor it. When I was seventeen years old, music had become my counselor when I needed help, my friend when I felt lonely, my father when I needed love, my pastor when I needed hope, and my lover when I needed to belong. That night, as I watched the B-52s dance their mess around on Saturday Night Live in a wacky, frenetic blur, I felt a connection and realized I would never live a regular existence. I was not meant to blend into the sleepy suburban streets of Springfield, Virginia, like another trench coat at the bus stop. I was born to fly my freak flag and cherish all of life's wonderful idiosyncrasies. I needed to break away from the routine.

Another memory, another step through the crossing.

With my mother's approval, I was let go. She recognized my purpose and gave me the freedom to roam wherever I wanted. Life quickly became a survival lesson, and my house was a hard floor, but I was LIVING, and music provided my sustenance when there was none. With my feet up on the dashboard, I watched the world pass by through a dirty windshield and learned to surrender to the unpredictability of a life without design, to rely on a road map with no destination, letting it take me wherever it might lead, never knowing what was around the next corner but faithfully relying on the music to keep me alive in the event that everything fell apart and I had to start again.

And I started over.

It seems like only yesterday that I was spending those long evenings on that unclean couch in Olympia, Washington, snuggled away in my sleeping bag thousands of miles from home, waiting for my next dream. I was a stranger in a stranger's house once more, but the ringing in my ears from the sound we produced together in that little barn outside of town lulled me to sleep every night and kept my fire going. My trusty divining rod had guided me to yet another well, one so deep that it eventually overflowed and drowned us all. I was lost without a lifeboat.

I could've sunk. I could've given up. I could've gone home. However, capitulation was never in my DNA.

As I heard the room next door fill up with the typical parade of after-show attendees, I composed myself and prepared to join them. I could hear their voices, and I recognized everyone. These were the voices of those who had supported me throughout these years. An extended family has become my new tribe.

I walked into the room and found Gus Brandt handing out drinks and passes, always doing his best to make everyone feel welcome in our chaotic little world. Gus had been my therapist, big brother, and bodyguard for decades, dealing with anything from broken guitars to shattered limbs. He had become my beacon when I felt lost in a sea of strangers, my refuge when I needed it, and I could always confide in him about my deepest struggles. Though he was not a musician, his passion for music was as strong, if not more so, than mine, and without his support, I would never make it to the next song, city, or stage. He is constantly present, and I am thankful for his protection.

Rami Jaffee, my trusted confidant, was floating around the room with the ease and nonchalance of a gypsy maître d', spreading his aura as the true "good times" ambassador of the Foo Fighters. Though he was hidden away in the corner of the stage every night, his contributions to the band over the years had proven vital, and he had added a musicality that had propelled us to new heights record after album. But, in addition to his musical abilities, his companionship had become a source of joy every day, a welcome break from the routine of life on the road. And each night, once the curtains have closed and the crowd has gone home, Rami and I will board our shared tour bus and drink, smoke, and dance as we speed down the highway to our next destination. Though he joined the band a decade later, he was truly one of us from the start, and I am grateful for his comfort.

There was Chris Shiflett, the man who came to our band's rescue when we were without a guitarist and in desperate need of musical help. Though our paths had crossed coincidentally at a Scream gig in Santa Barbara ten years prior to his fateful audition (the only time we had ever attempted such a thing), we had lived parallel lives up until that point, playing in punk rock bands with friends and living out of vans on pennies, with music and adventure being the only true rewards. Before he had played a note, I knew he'd be a fantastic fit because he'd enjoy every moment of being in this band, and I appreciate his gratitude.

Taylor Hawkins, my brother from another mother, my best friend, and a man I would take a bullet for, ripped through the room like an F5 tornado of hyperactive delight. Our kinship was instant when we first met, and it became stronger with each day, song, and note we played together. I am not hesitant to admit that our unexpected meeting was like love at first sight, creating a musical "twin flame" that still burns today. We've become an irrepressible duo, both onstage and off, seeking any and all adventure we can find. We were meant to be, and I am thankful that we discovered each other in this lifetime.

Nate Mendel was my voice of reason, my barometer, the one I could always rely on when I needed to be grounded. If it hadn't been for that unexpected encounter at my Thanksgiving meal in 1994, hunched around a Ouija board to communicate with the spirits of my haunted house in Seattle, the world would never have known the Foo Fighters we know today. We had developed this thing together from the ground up, overcome numerous difficulties, and remained pretty intact. Though I rarely express it, his presence in my life is essential, and I am not sure what I would do without him. I appreciate his dedication and loyalty.

Then there was Pat Smear. The man who was originally my punk rock hero and later became not only a bandmate twice, but also a reliable pillar in my life. Pat has always been there to walk through the fire with me, no matter the highs or lows, since he walked into Nirvana's rehearsal space in 1993 and gave the band another year of life. He was always present throughout my most difficult times, and with his wisdom and wit, he reassured me that I could overcome anything. That WE could get through anything. I hoped we'd be shoulder to shoulder from the first time we met, and I've been happy to stand in his shadow ever since. Every night onstage, when I look to my left and see the heavy plumes of smoke streaming from his smile, I feel safe, and I am eternally grateful for his kind and wise spirit.

As a group, we had each become a whirring wheel in a deafening clock, ticking only when the spinning teeth of one gear met those of another, locking us into coordinated movement. Without it, our pendulum would halt. The revolving door that had formerly plagued our early years was now locked, and we had become a permanent entity. Once in, you're in for good. The stability and security that we had all sought as divorced and rebellious teenagers might now be found in a bombardment of distorted guitars and laser-lit shows. We'd become a family.

My beautiful wife, Jordyn, the mother of my children, the queen of my life, the weight in my scale that keeps the arm from tipping, was holding court in the far corner of the room, holding a glass of champagne in her delicate hand. Our paths had met at a moment when I believed I was bound to live in the past indefinitely, but her courage and clarity provided me a way forward. We worked together to produce my family, which is my greatest success. My appreciation for life evolved alongside our family. With each child born, I was born anew, and with each step they took, I traced my own. Violet, Harper, and Ophelia gave me life in exchange, and I am grateful beyond words. Fatherhood trumped every hope, wish, or song I'd ever written, and as the years passed, I realized the true meaning of love. I no longer live solely for myself; I live for them.

However, the voices that could not be heard were possibly the most audible in the room.

I believed Jimmy should have been here. He was the first person I played my Naked Raygun record for when I returned home from a trip to Chicago in 1982, and the instant we dropped the needle on that primitive slab of vinyl, we launched on a new musical journey together as allies in the unconventional world of punk rock. We were two outliers in a sea of uniformity who invented our own culture, language, and cosmos via our fixation with music. No matter how strange I was, he always understood me and accepted my craziness, just as I did his. I looked up to him as the older brother I never had, and he influenced so much of who I am now. We were inseparable, having done everything together our entire lives, and it crushed my heart that I couldn't enjoy this moment with him. But deep down, I knew Dad would have valued this win since it belonged to both of us.

My father once told me, "This will never last," and it's possible that this challenge motivated me to make sure it did. We had battled to connect for our entire lives, yet even in his absence, his presence impacted me, for better or worse. I had long since let go of any bitterness toward him and forgiven him for his inadequacies as a parent, which eventually lightened the load of our relationship and allowed us to become wonderful friends. As his child, I inherited more than just fundamental physical traits from him: we shared the same hands, knees, and arms. I have to think that my talent to discern sound and play music by ear was inherited from his wonderful genetic code, and I had to thank him for this most valuable gift. Something dad was sure to recognize when I grew into a man.

I know he would have been proud, and I wish he were still here to complete this cycle with me.

And Kurt.

If only he had realized the joy that his music provided to the world, he might have discovered his own. Kurt affected my life in ways I never had the opportunity to express while he was still with us, and not thanking him for that is a regret I'll have to live with until we're reunited. I don't go a day without thinking about our time together, and when we meet in my dreams, I always feel happy and tranquil, like if he's only hiding and waiting to return.

Though they are no longer with us, I still carry these individuals in my heart wherever I go, just as they once did for me, and it is their faces that I see every night just before the house lights go out and I am greeted with a scream of applause. It belongs to them just as much as to me. Had they simply hung on a little longer, I wondered if they would have joined in this celebration, another reunion of lifetime friends linked by years of deep connection.

But standing in the center of it all was the undeniable matriarch of this extended family, the lady to whom all forty thousand screaming fans had just sung "Happy Birthday" earlier that night: my mother. As she stood on the stage beside me, the entire stadium erupted in thunderous chorus, I was overcome with emotion, knowing that this woman who had worked tirelessly to raise two children on her own—struggling to make ends meet, working multiple jobs, living paycheck to paycheck—and devoted her entire life to the benefit of others as a public school teacher was finally receiving the recognition she deserved. It goes without saying that none of us would have been present if not for her. She had given me life not once, but twice, by giving me the freedom to be who I wanted to be, eventually freeing me to follow my own destiny. Her faith in me gave me the bravery and confidence to believe in myself. She taught me to live with my own passion and conviction by sharing hers. And her unconditional love for me taught me how to love others unconditionally. She could've given up. She could've gone home. However, surrender was never in her DNA either.

She was always my hero and biggest inspiration; I owed everything to her.

That crosswalk had taken a lifetime to complete, but I was grateful for every step, still that same little boy with a guitar and a dream. Because I'm still unaware that I've aged. My mind and emotions continue to play a cruel joke on me, tricking me with the illusion of youth as I greet the world every day with the idealistic, mischievous eyes of a rebellious child seeking adventure and magic. Even the most basic and simple things continue to bring me joy and admiration. And as I accumulate more small lines and scars, I still wear them with pride, as if they are a trail of breadcrumbs thrown across a route that I will one day rely on to find my way back to where I began.

My tears had dried, and I gently entered the room on my two damaged crutches, only to be greeted with a large communal embrace. The circle was now complete, and we had all crossed the street together, glad for life, music, and the people we care about.

AND SURVIVAL.

The contents of this book may not be copied, reproduced or transmitted without the express written permission of the author or publisher. Under no circumstances will the publisher or author be responsible or liable for any damages, compensation or monetary loss arising from the information contained in this book, whether directly or indirectly. .

Disclaimer Notice:

Although the author and publisher have made every effort to ensure the accuracy and completeness of the content, they do not, however, make any representations or warranties as to the accuracy, completeness, or reliability of the content. , suitability or availability of the information, products, services or related graphics contained in the book for any purpose. Readers are solely responsible for their use of the information contained in this book

Every effort has been made to make this book possible. If any omission or error has occurred unintentionally, the author and publisher will be happy to acknowledge it in upcoming versions.

Copyright © 2024

All rights reserved.

Printed in Great Britain
by Amazon